Paddling
Okefenokee
National Wildlife Refuge

David M. O'Neill
and Elizabeth Anne Domingue

FALCON®

HELENA, MONTANA

A FALCON GUIDE®

Falcon® Publishing is continually expanding its list of recreational guidebooks. All books include detailed descriptions, accurate maps, and all the information necessary for enjoyable trips. You can order extra copies of this book and get information and prices for other Falcon® guidebooks by writing Falcon, P.O. Box 1718, Helena, MT 59624, or calling toll-free 1-800-582-2665. Also, please ask for a free copy of our current catalog. Visit our website at www.falconguide.com.

© 1998 by Falcon® Publishing, Inc., Helena, Montana.
Printed in the United States of America.

1 2 3 4 5 6 7 8 9 0 MG 03 02 01 00 99 98

Falcon and FalconGuide are registered trademarks of Falcon® Publishing, Inc.

Cover photo by O'Neill and O'Neill.
Book photos by O'Neill and O'Neill.

Library of Congress Cataloging-in-Publication Data.
O'Neill, David, 1964–
    Paddling Okefenokee National Wildlife Refuge / by David O'Neill
and Elizabeth Domingue.
        p.   cm. — (A FalconGuide)
    ISBN 1-56044-613-7 (pbk. : alk. paper)
    1. Canoes and canoeing—Okefenokee National Wildlife Refuge (Ga.
and Fla.)—Guidebooks.   2. Okefenokee National Wildlife Refuge (Ga.
and Fla.)—Guidebooks.   I. Domingue, Elizabeth, 1965–
II. Title.   III. Series: Falcon guide.
GV776.O54O54   1998
917.58'7520443—dc21   98-42199
                                                                CIP

CAUTION

Outdoor recreational activities are by their very nature potentially hazardous. All participants in such activities must assume responsibility for their own actions and safety. The information contained in this guidebook cannot replace sound judgment and good decision-making skills, which help reduce risk exposure, nor does the scope of this book allow for disclosure of all the potential hazards and risks involved in such activities.

Learn as much as possible about the outdoor recreational activities in which you participate, prepare for the unexpected, and be cautious. The reward will be a safer and more enjoyable experience.

 Text pages printed on recycled paper.

*To those who appreciate the value of all things
wild and pursue the long, hard journey of
protecting our remaining wilderness*

Contents

Acknowledgments

Special thanks to Cyndy Loftin and the Cooperative Fish and Wildlife Research Unit of the United States Geological Survey at the University of Florida for too many things to list. The very idea for this guidebook came as David was wading knee-deep in the Okefenokee muck while working for Cyndy and the CFWRU. Cyndy and the CFWRU were also instrumental in the creation of the trail maps by graciously allowing the use of their classified satellite image, maps, and facilities. We feel the value of this guidebook is greatly enhanced with the inclusion of these maps.

Thanks also to Sara Aicher, Judy Drury, and the rest of the staff at the Okefenokee National Wildlife Refuge for patiently answering our many questions and otherwise assisting our efforts in creating this guide. With Jim Burkhart and Maggie O'Connell, Sara also undertook the tedious task of reviewing the guidebook manuscript. Many thanks to each of them. We are also grateful to the Okefenokee National Wildlife Refuge for allowing the use of their vertebrate species lists to create the one included in the appendix.

Beth Hardee of Gainesville Fire Rescue and Kent Vliet of the University of Florida provided helpful comments on the first-aid and alligator safety sections, respectively. We thank them for their generous assistance.

Thanks also to Chris Stamper and Tony Moore for their work on the maps, and to Ann Owen for editing the manuscript.

Finally, we thank Falcon Publishing, especially Ric Bourie, Arik Ohnstad, and Randall Green, for making this guidebook possible.

Vicinity Map

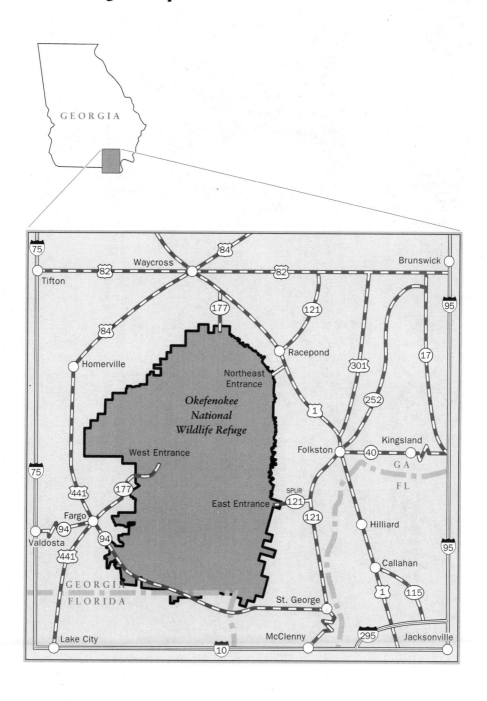

Pond Cypress trees along the Middle Fork of the Suwannee River.

Introduction

Paddling the Okefenokee Swamp is one of the Southeast's great canoeing experiences. In the Okefenokee you can pass quietly beneath grand, moss-cloaked cypresses; cross expansive, flower-covered marshes; and float lazy stretches of the Suwannee River. You can day-paddle from any of four major access points or embark on multiday excursions deep into the heart of the swamp. Much of the ecosystem is protected by the 396,315-acre Okefenokee National Wildlife Refuge, and the refuge maintains 110 miles of canoeable waterways. This guide was created to enhance your canoeing or kayaking experience within this natural treasure. It provides trail descriptions for the designated overnight canoe trips and day-use areas administered by the refuge. It also provides information on access points, safety, wildlife viewing, facilities, and general conditions. It does not provide information about the privately operated Okefenokee Swamp Park in the northern portion of the swamp or supplant regulatory information provided by the refuge.

Note: Our occasional use of the term canoe to refer to both canoe and kayak collectively is only a matter of convenience. It is not meant to imply that kayaks are less suitable for use in the Okefenokee. Our humblest apologies are offered in advance to devout kayakers who would never refer to their fine crafts as canoes.

GENERAL CONDITIONS

At first thought you might expect the Okefenokee Swamp to occupy the low bottomlands of a large river drainage where the water from a number of tributaries spreads and fills a wide plain. Somewhat surprisingly to the contrary, the Okefenokee Swamp lies in a relatively high, sandy basin in southern Georgia with a small section crossing into northern Florida. Little topographic relief exists across much of the expanse, and the area acts as an immense catch basin that collects rainwater, then slowly releases it. The net result is the development of an extensive, shallow wetland that provides favorable conditions for the growth of a variety of water-loving plants, such as Pond Cypress, sedges, and Fragrant Water Lily. About three-quarters of the Okefenokee's water is returned to the atmosphere through evapotranspiration. Almost all of the remaining water flows out along the Okefenokee's southern and western borders. Most of this drainage is through the Suwannee River to the Gulf of Mexico. The rest is carried by the St. Marys River to the Atlantic Ocean.

Understanding the delicate interplay of topography and rainfall is the key to understanding the Okefenokee and the paddling experience. Much of the Okefenokee is covered by shallow, virtually still waters. The main exceptions are areas of the Suwannee River drainage in the western portions of the swamp, where slow to moderate currents are encountered in some river and creek channels. Even in these drainages you can travel upstream against the current, though many prefer downstream routes, which take advantage of the slow southwestward flow. Nowhere in the swamp will you encounter fast water, and in very few places will you encounter noticeable currents. Most of the time you will be relying on your own paddling strength to traverse the swamp.

Extensive forests of Pond Cypress, Loblolly Bay, Black Gum, and Red Maple cover a large proportion of the Okefenokee. Far from presenting a uniform covering, this mix of trees settles over the swamp like an immense flock of birds; lone sentinels, scattered clumps, and sprawling congregations stand apart from expansive woodlands. Beneath the canopy, and at times covering large acreages itself, is a well-developed shrub community of which the predominate members are the glossy-leaved Hurrah Bush, the sun-loving Titi, and the richly named Poor-man's Soap. Where the sandy floor of the swamp basin rises to form dry-soiled islands, such as Billys to the west and Blackjack to the south, the lowland swamp forest gives way to stands of Slash Pine, Longleaf Pine, and Saw Palmetto.

Most unexpected in the Okefenokee's swampy landscape is the occurrence of open, sunlit, shallow marshes called prairies. These openings are often reminiscent of shrubby wet-meadows and are vegetated by a variety of hydrophytic (water-loving) plants. The shallower portions are dominated by thickly growing, emergent sedges, grasses, and forbs; Maidencane, Walter's Sedge, beakrushes, yellow-eyed grasses, and Redroot are common. In the deeper water, long-stemmed and floating plants like Fragrant Water Lily, Spatterdock, bladderworts, and Neverwet predominate.

Prairie and islands in the Okefenokee Swamp.

CULTURAL HISTORY

Use of the Okefenokee Swamp by humans has been quite varied over the centuries, though parts of this cultural history are poorly documented and leave us with mysteries to ponder. How typical of the Okefenokee.

Much speculation has been made regarding the identity of the early aboriginal inhabitants. In 1773, William Bartram was informed by Native Americans that the "Ouaquaphenogaw" was inhabited by "the posterity of a fugitive remnant of the ancient Yamases, who escaped massacre after a conflict with the Creek Nation." Even today, detailed information on early human presence in the swamp region is scarce due to the lack of properly excavated archaeological sites and thus a dearth of artifacts. Many or most of the burial mounds left by the natives have been dug up by curious and somewhat oblivious white visitors.

Paleo-Indians arrived to the vicinity of the Okefenokee during the late Pleistocene or early Holocene (prior to 8000 B.C.) and were probably the first human inhabitants of the area. These initial occupants were followed by people of four succeeding cultural traditions, Archaic (8000–1000 B.C.), Woodland (1000 B.C.–A.D. 900), Mississippian (A.D. 900 to the time of European contact), and Historic (from the time of European contact to the present).

The Archaic occupation is poorly understood. The earliest known artifact found in the Okefenokee dates from 4000 B.C. The next period, the Woodland, likely saw the most intensive use of the swamp by Native Americans. Settlements were established and burial mounds built on most of the large islands within the swamp and at many places on its perimeter between A.D. 500 and A.D. 1000. The scarcity of ceramics from the Mississippian Period suggest that permanent or semipermanent settlements were absent then, though the swamp likely was used as a hunting and collecting area. Occupation of the swamp by Seminoles began in, or soon after, 1750. Seminole villages existed on Billys, Floyds, and Mitchell islands. During the Second Seminole War in 1838, General Charles Floyd marched through the swamp to flush out the remaining holdouts. On Billys Island he found an extensive village—recently abandoned. However, Floyd did not succeed in capturing the Seminoles since they had already escaped to the Everglades.

The first settlers of European descent to live in the swamp were the Lee and Chesser families. The Swampers, as they were called, lived in the swamp isolated from mainstream America from the 1850s through the 1940s. The Swampers made their living off of the abundant supply of game and fish, supplemented by the crops they raised. They also traded furs, game, and cane syrup for other staples that they obtained from merchants outside of the swamp.

In September of 1891, Captain Harry Jackson began his Suwannee Canal project—the draining of the swamp for agricultural purposes. The canal was dug 45 feet wide by 6 feet deep at 3 miles per year by the Suwannee Canal Company. After losing a great deal of money and realizing that the waters of the Suwannee Canal were running back into the swamp instead of out, canal construction was

The tin-roofed cabin on Floyds Island has a fireplace to keep occupants warm.

abandoned. Thirteen miles had been completed. General Henry Jackson (Harry's father) began a timber harvesting project to regain some of the fortune lost to the swamp. However, this endeavor failed as well. And so in 1897 the Jackson era in the swamp ended.

Next in line to exploit the swamp was the Hebard Lumber Company. They purchased 295,671 acres of the swamp and began cutting its timber in 1909. The primary species of interest was cypress. However, they also logged pine from all of the islands and took bay and gum from within the swamp. The Hebard Lumber Company built an efficient railroad system throughout the swamp to gain access to the trees. The Company had permanent (main) swamp lines with temporary (spur) lines branching out to the cypress bays. Over an 18-year period they harvested nearly one-half billion cubic meters of timber and turned a profit of over $1,000,000. They stopped the logging operation in 1927 only because the timber ran out.

The Okefenokee National Wildlife Refuge was established on March 30, 1937, largely through the efforts of the Okefenokee Preservation Society. Our deepest gratitude extends to all those persons who, so long ago, recognized the unique value of the Okefenokee and sought to protect it. The 396,315-acre refuge encompasses approximately 80 percent of the swamp. It is administered by the Fish and Wildlife Service, United States Department of the Interior. Refuge personnel seek "to manage the Okefenokee National Wildlife Refuge as an integral component of the greater Okefenokee ecosystem by restoring and maintaining native flora and fauna and associated natural processes, and by providing educational and compatible recreational opportunities." In 1974, 353,981 acres of the refuge were designated as a national wilderness area.

WEATHER

The weather of the Okefenokee is typical of the inland regions of the southeastern coastal plain with variable winters and hot, humid summers. Spring and fall provide an abundance of cool nights and warm, sunny days. Keep in mind that summer hot spells often last through September and spring warm-ups can begin as early as late February.

Despite seemingly mild average temperatures, some winter days are surprisingly cold, whereas others decidedly springlike. Cold fronts routinely cause temperatures to drop into the 20s. (The record low is 4 degrees F.) Preparing for a variety of conditions will keep you most comfortable.

Summer weather is the most extreme, combining high temperatures, high humidity, and strong sunshine. Broad-brimmed hats, light clothing, sunscreen, and plenty of water should accompany every summer traveler. Also remember to pack reliable rain gear during this time, as almost half of the Okefenokee's rainfall occurs during afternoon thunderstorms in June through September.

Temperature and Rainfall Data for Suwannee Canal Recreation Area

Month	Average Minimum, degrees F	Average Maximum, degrees F	Average Precipitation, inches
January	45	68	3.5
February	46	71	3.48
March	50	77	4.24
April	53	82	3.34
May	61	88	3.96
June	67	92	5.9
July	70	94	7.75
August	70	93	7.15
September	67	90	5.22
October	58	81	3.22
November	47	75	2.21
December	43	67	2.84

WATER LEVELS

Typically, ample water is available for canoeing on all of the trails throughout the year. However, since the Okefenokee depends greatly on rainfall to maintain its water levels, periodic droughts can cause trails to become impassable. During these times, refuge personnel close these trails and cancel trip permits affected by the closure. Though it is not a common occurrence, it is a possibility for which you should be prepared. Even if you are not contacted by refuge personnel about a trail closure, it is a good idea to ask about current water conditions in the swamp before your visit.

In general, water levels are highest in early spring (February through mid-April) and late summer, then decline as the thunderstorms diminish at the end of summer. October, November, and December are often the driest months and the most likely to include trail closings or difficult passages due to low water. Be forewarned: These trends are long-term averages. In any particular year water levels do just as they please, and summer droughts, which are not uncommon, can completely reverse the usual trends.

Also be aware that trails following the river and creek drainages on the western side of the swamp are more prone to low or insufficient water levels than those wandering the prairies in the east. Especially susceptible are the Brown Trail and the Orange Trail between Canal Run and Stephen C. Foster State Park. On the other hand, the most reliable sections of trail are those that rely upon the less

Average Annual Water Levels
Okefenokee National Wildlife Refuge

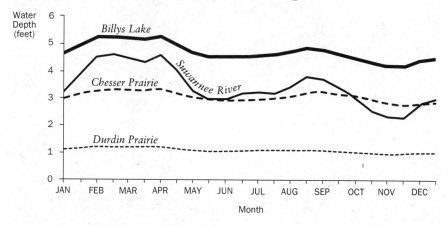

variable water levels of the prairies. For instance, water levels in Durdin Prairie vary less than one-half foot in an average year, whereas those of the Suwannee River vary by 2 feet or more. The deeper waters of Billys Lake and the Suwannee Canal become inaccessible only during the most severe droughts.

TRAILS AND TRAIL MARKERS

Within the refuge you will encounter three major types of canoe trails. The widest and deepest trails follow the paths of major canals that were built within the swamp during past lumbering and dredging operations. These trails are typically 10 or more yards wide, 5 to 7 feet deep, and predominantly free of aquatic vegetation. Narrower and shallower are the winding boat trails that snake across much of the swamp. These trails are typically 2 to 3 yards wide and 2 to 4 feet deep. Although they are periodically maintained by a trailcutter boat (about as strange a craft as you will see), they have a tendency to fill with aquatic vegetation, especially by late summer. This can make them more difficult to paddle because the dense vegetation pulls on your canoe. The third type of trail, and the only natural one, is the river and creek channels of the Suwannee River drainage. These trails are as varied as the river drainage itself and can be broad and sweeping or narrow and winding. The central portions of the channels are generally free of vegetation and the currents quite lazy (0 to 2 miles per hour).

To aid in navigation the refuge maintains a system of trail markers, which includes PVC pipes, white-tipped markers, and signs. The trails of the designated overnight canoe trips also have colored markers and mileage figures that correspond to each of the six color-coded trails (Red, Green, Blue, Purple, Orange, and Brown). Some day-use trails do not have trail markers, but are generally easy to follow. A number of wooden signs mark trail junctions and provide direction to major features.

A trail marker indicates mile 16 along the Orange Trail.

The only portage in the refuge is the 0.3-mile portage on the Green Trail across Floyds Island.

DRINKING AND WASH WATER

Even though the Okefenokee Swamp is a freshwater wetland and you will be virtually surrounded by water, you will still need to pack in all the water that you need on your trip. In addition to the usual hazards, such as protozoa and bacteria, the swamp's water has some particular ones that make it difficult to properly treat by traditional boiling or filtering methods. To begin with, the water in the swamp is heavily stained by the natural tannins that leach from decaying vegetation. Some people find the bitter taste and discoloration unappealing. More troubling is the flocculent, peaty substrate of the swamp. The slightest disturbance causes it to disperse through the water column, mixing the water with an abundance of fine organic matter and the highly irritating spicules of freshwater sponges. This debris quickly clogs your nifty, fifty- or one-hundred-dollar water filter. Then there is the mercury contamination; though the water has not been specifically tested for human safety, mercury levels in some of the Okefenokee's fish have been found to exceed Environmental Protection Agency standards.

In calculating the amount of water to take on your trip, keep in mind that your daily drinking water requirements depend on a variety of factors, including weather, amount of physical exertion, and your size, age, and acclimation to hot environments. Experience helps in determining how much to bring, but there are some guidelines that will get you in the ballpark. Use a base figure of 4 quarts of drinking water per person per day (24 hours), then adjust the amount for the anticipated conditions. Summer travelers on long, strenuous routes should consider carrying one and one-half to two times that amount. Those on less strenuous trips during milder weather may be able to get by with a little less. Also, don't forget to include extra water for any food preparation that you have planned.

Depending on circumstances, you may want to carry additional water for your washing needs as well. The tannins and suspended particulates in the swamp water can make it difficult to use even as wash water. However, if you decide to bring only drinking water, then try to obtain your wash water in an area of deep, open water. It is also wise to avoid areas of concentrated human use. Don't do your washing in the swamp itself. Instead, carry the water back to camp for washing, then dispose of the dirty water in the toilet, as you should all waste water. A small wash basin makes these tasks much easier. Do not use untreated swamp water for washing chores in which there is a risk of ingestion.

Carrying your water in several small containers is wiser than using a single large one. Water containers, especially the less-durable collapsible varieties, are apt to spring leaks. If all your water is in one badly leaking container, you will have to come up with some ingenious field repairs in a hurry.

If you must obtain emergency drinking water directly from the swamp, use as many of the following procedures as possible. Obtain your water from an area of deep, open water, avoiding areas of concentrated human use. Try to minimize the amount of disturbance in the immediate area while gathering the water. Filter or strain the water through a clean piece of cloth or clothing as many times as necessary to remove particulate matter, then purify the water by putting it through a water purification filter, boiling for at least five minutes, or adding water purification tablets.

You can fill your water containers from faucets at the Suwannee Canal Recreation Area and Stephen C. Foster State Park. The Kingfisher Landing and Suwannee River Sill Recreation Area access points do not provide water services.

THE WILDERNESS EXPERIENCE

Officially, 353,981 acres of the refuge are designated as a national wilderness area. This might lead you to envision a trackless wilderness devoid of motorized vehicles, manmade structures, and roads. To be sure, much of the Okefenokee is trackless wilderness. However, in order to provide access to the swamp, the refuge administers a system of boat trails, composting toilets, and campsites across the wilderness area. And in order to facilitate maintenance, monitoring, and research activities, refuge personnel and other co-operators regularly use a variety of powerboats within the wilderness. In addition, a large proportion of the boat trails in the designated wilderness are open to public motorboat use.

All of these factors can lead to a less than pristine wilderness experience. However, if you are prepared for the possibility of sharing a portion of the trail with a few motorboats or the occasional airboat, these occurrences should seem more like minor nuisances than intolerable trespasses. To give you an idea of what to expect, we have included a few notes in the descriptions about the level and type of use that particular trails and access points receive. Despite these drawbacks, the Okefenokee still offers one of the finest wilderness canoeing experiences in the Southeast. If you are a real solitude seeker, schedule your trip for the middle of the week during the off-season (June through September), leave the boat ramp early in the morning, and choose one of the least accessible overnight canoe trips.

LEAVE NO TRACE

Since much of the Okefenokee is a national wilderness area, it imposes added responsibility on the visitor. Proper wilderness etiquette should be practiced at all times. This means strict adherence to no-trace guidelines. Think of the Okefenokee as a great work of art—a natural masterpiece. Show your respect by minimizing your presence and impact in all ways. Take pride in your ability to pass through without a trace.

Never discard garbage or food scraps in the swamp no matter how small or insignificant they may seem. Make every effort to retrieve any items accidentally dropped overboard or off an overnight shelter, including that gum wrapper the wind snatched out of your hand and sent sailing behind you. Avoid disturbing wildlife (and other visitors) by keeping quiet and not approaching them too closely. Avoid disturbing plants and other natural features by leaving them in place and building fires only at designated sites. Deposit all human waste in a toilet. Flush toilets are available at the Suwannee Canal Recreation Area and Stephen C. Foster State Park. Composting toilets are provided at each overnight shelter and at a few other locations within the swamp. Campers on overnight canoe trips are required to use portable toilets between facilities. Waste wash water should be disposed of in the composting toilets and not directly into the swamp.

To dispose of portable toilet waste, empty the contents of the collection bag into a flush toilet when you return. The empty collection bag can then be placed in a garbage receptacle. Don't put toilet collection bags or other garbage in any of the composting or flush toilets. Campers using chemical portable toilets with formal-dehyde- or bleach-based solutions should refrain from emptying them in any of the composting toilets or flush toilets at the refuge. The chemicals disrupt the decompositional process of the composting toilets and septic-tank drain fields of the flush toilets.

Of course, these are just the basics. Even the best-intentioned person may un-wittingly transgress proper wilderness etiquette out of simple ignorance. Your best defense against such blunders is to keep up-to-date on the latest no-trace practices (refer to *Leave No Trace* by Will Harmon, published by Falcon, and other sources). Keeping the Okefenokee a natural treasure is everyone's responsibility. If you can do more than your share, we will all greatly appreciate it. Thanks in advance.

1. Refuge Permits and Regulations

If you will be limiting your canoeing in the Okefenokee to day tripping, you will not need to make special preparations. If you plan on participating in an overnight canoe trip, however, you will have to make advance reservations (see Permits, below). In either case take a minute to familiarize yourself with the appropriate regulations. Take special note of regulations regarding safety equipment, pets, swimming, alcohol consumption, and the protection of plants and wildlife.

PERMITS

The Okefenokee National Wildlife Refuge operates a series of overnight campsites within the interior of the swamp as part of their system of designated overnight canoe trips. Camping at these sites is limited to a single group per site per day, thereby greatly enhancing the wilderness experience of the Okefenokee. If you are interested in taking an overnight canoe trip in the refuge, you will need to make a reservation and obtain a permit by calling the refuge headquarters at 912-496-3331 on weekdays, excluding holidays, between 7 A.M. and 10 A.M. eastern time. A fee is charged based on the number of nights and number of people in the party. Though reservations will not be taken after 10 A.M., you may still call after that time to request information. Reservations for trips are taken up to two months in advance of the intended departure date. At times trips get booked within minutes

A bird's-eye view of the Bluff Lake shelter on the Green Trail.

of becoming available, so it is wise to make your reservations as early as possible and have alternative choices ready. During the high use periods of March and April, special restrictions are in effect. During that time you will be limited to a single trip per year with a maximum stay of two nights.

Permits are not required for day-use canoeing or kayaking.

CANOE TRIP CAMPSITES

Most of the designated overnight canoe trips provide elevated wooden platforms for above-water campsites. Each is approximately 20 feet by 28 feet and partially roofed. However, the Cravens Hammock and Floyds Island stops offer sufficient dry land and are therefore not equipped with shelters. On Cravens Hammock you simply find a suitable spot in the woods and make your camp. On Floyds Island you can pitch your tent in the woods or stay in the small cabin on the island. The Canal Run campsite lies on the spoil bank of the Suwannee Canal and is somewhat of a hybrid. It has a small, 10 foot by 20 foot platform and a bit of dry ground.

Open fires are permitted only at Cravens Hammock, Floyds Island, and Canal Run. Fire rings are provided at these sites. Every campsite is equipped with a composting toilet.

Refuge regulations allow as many as 20 people per group on the designated overnight canoe trips. Unless you will be camping on Floyds Island or Cravens Hammock, this will make for very crowded conditions. Pitching seven or eight tents on a 20-foot by 28-foot platform is unrealistic. If you are using backpacker-style, two-person tents, a more reasonable number is three or four.

REGULATIONS

The Okefenokee National Wildlife Refuge is administered by the United States Fish and Wildlife Service. Stephen C. Foster State Park is operated within the refuge by the Georgia Department of Natural Resources through a cooperative agreement. Adhering to the following list of refuge and park regulations will help keep you out of trouble, ensure a safe visit, and protect the ecosystem.

1. Disturbing or collecting plants or animals is prohibited.
2. Feeding or harassing wildlife is prohibited.
3. Pets must be kept on a 10-foot leash and are not permitted in public buildings or boats. Within Stephen C. Foster State Park, pets are only allowed in campsites and must be on a 6-foot leash. Nowhere within the refuge are pets allowed in the swamp.
4. Littering is prohibited.
5. Refuge travel is restricted to designated areas during posted hours.
6. Each boat occupant is required to have a Coast Guard approved personal floatation device (PFD). Children ten-years-old and younger must wear their PFDs at all times while in a boat.
7. Outboard motors are limited to 10-horsepower or less.

8. Camping is permitted only on overnight canoe trips and at designated areas in Stephen C. Foster State Park.
9. Fires are permitted in designated areas only.
10. Swimming is prohibited in refuge waters.
11. Firearms and other weapons are prohibited on the refuge except during designated hunts.
12. Fishing is permitted in accordance with Georgia State fishing laws.
13. The use of live minnows or trotlines for fishing is prohibited.
14. Bicycling is permitted on the wildlife observation drive and in Stephen C. Foster State Park. Georgia state law requires all bicyclists to wear a helmet.
15. All state, federal, and county laws regarding alcohol consumption are enforced. County regulations prohibit public intoxication.
16. All licenses, permits, equipment, and effects, including vehicles and canoes, are subject to inspection by state and federal officers.

Participants in overnight canoe trips must also adhere to the following additional regulations.
1. All parties engaging in overnight canoe trips must obtain a permit.
2. Group size is limited to 20 people.
3. The canoe permit must be carried by the group leader, who is responsible for the party following all regulations.
4. Parties must launch from each site before 10 A.M. to ensure that the overnight stop is reached before dark.
5. Each canoe party must register when entering and leaving the swamp and at each overnight stop.
6. Motors of any kind are not permitted on canoe trips.
7. Hunting is prohibited.
8. You must remain at the designated overnight area between sunset and sunrise for only one night.
9. Open fires are permitted only at Canal Run, Floyds Island, and Cravens Hammock.
10. Camp stoves are required for cooking.
11. Each party is required to have a compass, map, flashlight, and portable toilet with disposable bags.
12. Follow exactly the route on your permit.
13. Do not stray from the assigned trail.
14. Only one party per stop allowed.
15. Any additions or changes to permits must be completed prior to departure.
16. Canoe permit fees do not include launch fees.
17. Unauthorized commercial guiding and outfitting is prohibited.
18. Parking placards showing your permit number must be displayed on the dashboard of any vehicle you leave parked overnight at any refuge entrance.
19. You may be held financially responsible for unnecessary rescues.

2. Hazards

While most canoeists and kayakers paddle the Okefenokee without mishap, you need to be aware of and prepared for potential hazards. Carry first-aid and survival kits (see "Checklist of Equipment and Supplies," page 24). Keep them secure and accessible, and know how to use them.

Before we discuss specific safety issues, a word of caution is in order. If you have little, or no, wilderness canoeing and camping experience, please seek additional resources for assistance. If you have special health limitations or conditions, you may need to make additional preparations and adjustments not discussed in this guide. This is not meant to discourage you from canoeing in the Okefenokee, but only to advise you to please make the proper preparations based on your individual skills and needs in order to insure that your canoeing experience is both enjoyable and safe.

Also keep in mind that the following safety tips are by no means comprehensive. They are provided to advise you of some prominent safety issues. Again, please seek additional resources for in-depth discussions. Four good sources are *Wild Country Companion* by Will Harmon, *The Outward Bound Wilderness First-Aid Handbook* by Jeff Isaac and Peter Goth, *Wilderness Medicine* by William Forgey, and *Wilderness Survival* by Suzanne Swedo. Each has a particular focus and approach. Another good source of information is the American Red Cross. In addition to standard first-aid courses, some Red Cross chapters offer wilderness first-aid courses, which address the specifics of administering first-aid in remote settings.

Above all, in the unlikely event that you find yourself in a potentially life-threatening situation, stay calm. If you keep your wits and apply yourself to the tasks at hand, your chances of a desirable outcome will improve.

The following is a list of elements and situations to be aware of when planning a trip in the swamp:

Airboats. Refuge staff and other officials regularly use airboats for transportation within the swamp. While many people are fascinated by this unusual mode of transportation, encountering one on the narrow, winding boat trails of the Okefenokee represents a potential hazard. You will probably hear the unmuffled roar of the airboat's engine from quite a distance. Use this to your advantage and move to an open section of trail, avoiding blind corners and narrow passages. If you have time, secure any loose items and protect equipment you want to keep dry from prop wash, the wet spray generated by the airboat's propeller. Then position yourself to one side of the trail, stop paddling, and make yourself as visible as possible. Wave your paddle in the air to gain the driver's attention if needed. The airboat driver should slow and pass. As the airboat passes, shield your face and eyes from the propwash at the rear. Finally, wait until the airboat is well past before resuming paddling.

Alligators. American Alligators have been basking in the sun, so to speak, for more than two million years, and many people travel to the Okefenokee hoping to get a glimpse of this triumph of existence. As with all large predators, however, some precautions are in order. Although they rarely attack humans, there are certain circumstances and times of the year when alligators present a genuine danger. This is particularly true from June through August, when female alligators are tending their eggs. The eggs are laid in nests that the females create by scraping plant debris into a large mound. Female alligators protect their nests and their young, so stay well clear of both.

A more serious problem occurs when people feed alligators, as these 'gators lose their fear of humans and learn to associate people with food. An alligator conditioned in this way is very dangerous. Never feed an alligator and avoid any that appear unafraid. Anglers should never string their catch in the water or trail it behind their canoe within easy reach of an opportunistic alligator. Campers at overnight shelters should hang their food and never discard food scraps in the water. Also keep in mind that alligators accustomed to people may allow a closer approach. Do not confuse their tolerance with tameness. They still remain wild animals, and you should maintain a respectable distance.

On occasion you may find an alligator uncomfortably close to or completely blocking your path. This is most likely to happen when an alligator hauls out to sun on the bank of a narrow section of trail. Avoid simply trying to pass quietly by an alligator in this situation. If the alligator suddenly feels threatened, it will likely dash to the safety of deep water by the most direct route. If the alligator does not feel threatened until you have paddled alongside, it may "escape" directly toward you. You can envision for yourself the possible outcomes of that scenario. Never position yourself in the path of an alligator's escape route to water.

If you can't detour around the alligator, you may be able to gently coax it out of your way. In many instances, diligent use of your paddle to lightly splash the alligator with water is sufficient. If more persuasion is required, call out and thump the ground with your paddle in combination with the splashing. Just remember to keep a safe distance and watch closely for any signs of aggressive or defensive behavior.

In rare instances, large groups of alligators congregate in the deeper water of the trails during drought. If you find your way blocked by one of these congregations, slowly herd the alligators down the trail in front of you from a safe distance, while calling out and using your paddle to splash them if needed. Be patient. They will eventually find a side pool or backwater and get out of your way. Dave once waited an hour for a raft of 50 or more alligators to work their way down the Brown Trail—an amazing experience.

Of course if you ever meet up with a large alligator or one that does not respond to gentle coaxing or seems aggressive or defensive in any way, immediately

The American Alligator is a long-time resident of the swamp.

back off. Yield the right-of-way, wait until it leaves of its own accord, turn around, or do whatever else you need to avoid a confrontation. Alligators hiss, open their jaws, and face directly toward you when feeling threatened. They also make sudden movements, often splashing about and slashing their tails. If an alligator displays any of these behaviors, you are too close.

Finally, everyone should be aware that alligators view pets and even children as prey. Do not allow either to wander near resting alligators or along shores. Certainly do not allow either to wade or swim in alligator-inhabited waters (swimming is prohibited in the refuge). And regardless of time of year or apparent temperament, always treat a large alligator with a great deal of respect. Their potential for harm is just too great.

Becoming lost. Once off-trail, there are surprisingly few prominent landmarks from which to regain your bearings in the Okefenokee. If you can, backtrack to the last point you knew you were on the trail. If that does not work and you definitely do not know where you are or where the trail is, stay put and wait for help. Rescue operations at the Okefenokee are typically done by boat and/or helicopter. Stay with your boat and signal from an unconcealed location, using the signal mirror, flares, and whistle from your survival kit. A series of three signals of any type is commonly recognized as a distress signal.

Signing in and out of the refuge's log books will greatly aid rescue efforts should you need them. Another good idea is to have a float-plan buddy (someone not on the trip with you) with whom you can leave a trip itinerary and whom you can inform of your safe return. This person can notify authorities if you are overdue (allowing for minor delays) and initiate a search as soon as possible. Conscientious use of these last two measures will not only help you if you are lost, but it will also reduce the likelihood of an unwarranted rescue effort being launched for which the refuge may hold you financially responsible.

Constricted passages. Some sections of trail in the Okefenokee are obstructed by overhanging branches, downed trees, submerged stumps and logs, masses of floating peat, aquatic vegetation, narrow banks, shallow water, or other obstacles. These sections of trail often require extra caution and effort to navigate. Submerged stumps and logs are difficult to see, and thus avoid, in the Okefenokee's dark water. A slow pace and stable paddling position (kneeling in some cases) is a wise precaution in areas prone to these obstacles.

Though obstructions are most likely to occur along the smaller boat trails and creek channels, you may occasionally encounter sections of trail anywhere within the swamp that are blocked or greatly constricted. At times, you may have to exit your canoe and drag or lift it across an obstruction. Be extremely careful; the peaty substrate of the swamp is often very unstable (see "Peat Quagmires," page 20).

Heat exhaustion and heat stroke. At times the sun burns down on the Okefenokee with such intensity that even the water can become hot enough to scald your feet. Heat exhaustion and heat stroke are real possibilities. Bring a broad-brimmed hat and be sure to drink plenty of water. Including a few salt tablets in the first-aid kit is a good idea, as is using an electrolyte replacement drink, such as Gatorade.

If you or anyone traveling with you develops symptoms of heat exhaustion—nausea, headache, dizziness, fast pulse, heavy breathing, weakness, or skin that is damp and pale—find a shady spot under some shrubs or trees, cool the affected person, provide water, and allow him or her to rest. Depending on circumstances, it may be wise to limit travel to the cooler hours of the day and/or suspend paddling duties of the affected person.

Victims of heat stroke (like those of heat exhaustion) may have a fast pulse and fast, shallow breathing. Also, their skin may be hot, red, and dry from an inability to sweat. More reliably though, heat stroke victims exhibit altered mental states (confused and/or erratic behavior) or lose consciousness. Suspect heat stroke in anyone behaving abnormally or irrationally on a hot day, especially in association with exercise. Heat stroke is a life-threatening emergency. The victim must be cooled immediately and given professional medical attention as soon as possible.

Of course, the best approach is to prevent any heat-related difficulties from happening in the first place. Two of the most effective measures are to drink plenty of water and to avoid strenuous activity during the hottest part of the day. Get an early start so that you can take a break, or slow your pace, during the heat of midday and drink at frequent, regular intervals before you become thirsty.

Hypothermia. So how cold can it get in southern Georgia? Is 4 degrees F cold enough? Typical winter lows range in the 30s and 40s—precisely the temperature range in which most cases of hypothermia occur. If for some reason you dump your boat or otherwise get wet at those temperatures, you could be in for trouble.

Keeping a discomfort from becoming a medical emergency will greatly depend on your ability to get dry and warm. A dry change of clothes, dry sleeping bag, and dry tent are essential, so make sure that these items are doubly sealed in waterproof containers (see "Keeping Your Gear Dry," page 26).

Symptoms of hypothermia include shivering, lethargy, drowsiness, slurred speech, impaired judgment, and decreased motor control. In advanced stages shivering ceases, and the affected person becomes uncooperative and loses consciousness. If anyone develops these symptoms in association with cold, wet, or windy conditions, you will need to take immediate action. Persons suffering from hypothermia may not realize that it is happening to them. Keep an eye on each other.

The main objective in treating hypothermia is to get the affected person warm, dry, and sheltered. In mild cases, get the affected person under shelter, replace wet clothes with dry ones, and add a warm hat. If appropriate have the person exercise to warm up. Alternatively, you may need to have the person get into a sleeping bag and drink warm (non-alcoholic) fluids—hot chocolate is a good choice. Make sure that you have placed an insulative pad underneath the sleeping bag. Bottles filled with heated water and wrapped to avoid direct contact can be placed in the bag to aid recovery. High energy foods—fruit, chocolate, etc.— will also help. In more severe cases it will be necessary to have one or two other persons (naked) get into the sleeping bag with the affected person (also naked except for a warm hat) and pile more sleeping bags on top. Do not attempt to give an uncooperative or unconscious person warm drinks or food. Severe cases of hypothermia require specific treatments, which are not discussed here. Handle them carefully and monitor them closely. Be ready to perform cardiopulmonary resuscitation if necessary.

One of the complicating factors in regard to hypothermia in the Okefenokee is the scarcity of dry, sheltered locations. You will have to use your best judgment when deciding whether to rig an impromptu shelter in your canoe (more difficult in a kayak), proceed quickly to the nearest dry land or shelter, or both. Treating hypothermia other than in your boat or at a developed site is not recommended under most circumstances. Trying to find a suitable, dry location amid the trees and shrubs in the swamp is an uncertain proposition at best. In addition to the great difficulty in finding such a spot, you may waste valuable time, slow rescue efforts, or even become lost. All of these outcomes will only exacerbate the situation. In determining the best course of action consider the distance to the closest dry land or shelter, the current and future weather conditions, and the severity of the symptoms. Keep in mind that there are a number of shelters located throughout the swamp in addition to the designated overnight stops.

Insects that bite (and their relatives). Mosquitoes and deer flies (locally known as yellow flies) are the most bothersome of the swamp's biting insects. Mosquitoes can be active at any time of the year during suitably warm weather, but are most numerous from April through October. Deer flies are at their worst from May through September. Commercially available repellents are reasonably effective.

However, at times the mosquitoes and deer flies are absolutely voracious, and repellents are not sufficient. This is when lightweight, loose-fitting, long-sleeved shirts and trousers offer better protection. Head nets and bug suits can increase your enjoyment during the height of the bug season. A tent with insect netting is highly recommended.

Chiggers and ticks are not usually much of a problem on canoe trips. You will most likely encounter them at put-ins and take-outs or as you are walking around at an island campsite. In regard to chiggers, avoid sitting or lying directly on the ground. With ticks you should take the normal precaution of regularly checking yourself and your clothes. Repellents can be used for extra protection from both. To remove a tick that has attached itself, use tweezers to grasp the tick at the attachment point on the skin, then slowly pull the tick out with a small bit of skin (just enough to ensure removal of the mouthparts). Wash the wound and give it a dab of antiseptic to help prevent infection. Be aware that Lyme disease and Rocky Mountain spotted fever occur in Georgia.

Insects that sting (and their relatives). Wasps and bees are active throughout the swamp during the warm months. Yellowjackets are often attracted to sweet drinks, food, perfumes, lotions, and bright colors. If you are bothered by them, avoid wearing brightly colored clothes or strong scents. Keep food and drinks inaccessible.

Several species of paper wasp are common in the wooded areas of the swamp. They often build their nests on the undersides of leaves and will sting when disturbed. Limiting contact with shrubby vegetation is the best defense, since the small nests are difficult to detect.

Scorpions are often found in the leaf litter and under debris in the upland areas of the swamp. Watch where you put your hands if you are picking up objects on the ground.

Fire Ants occur throughout the swamp but are most prevalent in the dry, upland areas. Their painful bites, stings, and subsequent welts are not soon forgotten, especially since they usually entail the simultaneous attack of an entire battalion. Stay clear of their conspicuous mounds and you should avoid any problems.

If you're allergic to insect stings, consult a doctor and consider carrying a doctor-prescribed, anaphylactic shock kit. Allergic reactions to insect stings tend to increase in severity with repeated exposure and can be life threatening. They are difficult to treat without proper medications. If you are unsure whether you are allergic to insect stings or have ever suffered even a mild allergic reaction, talk with a doctor before your trip. Antihistamines such as Benadryl can provide relief in mild cases.

Motorboats. Motorboat operators are allowed to travel many of the same trails as canoeists and kayakers. When encountering one it is best to yield the right-of-way, pull to the side, and allow them to pass. Keep in mind that many of the motorboat operators in the Okefenokee are rather inexperienced, sometimes renting a motorboat for the first time. Give them a little extra room and overlook minor discourtesies. However, if you are approached by a boat that you feel is traveling too fast or is otherwise endangering your craft, do not hesitate to signal the driver (politely, of course) to slow down or alter course.

Nuisance wildlife. The Raccoon is your most likely camp pilferer. Intelligent, persistent, stealthy, agile, and surprisingly strong, they can be difficult to thwart. Try to keep food smells contained in plastic and hang unattended gear out of their reach as best you can. Keeping a clean camp will greatly reduce the chance of attracting one of these camp robbers or creating trouble for those who follow.

Black Bears also occur in the Okefenokee. Though there has never been a report of a Black Bear bothering campers in the Okefenokee, you don't want to be the first. As with Raccoons, suppressing food odors and keeping your gear inaccessible is your best defense.

Peat quagmires. The oxygen-poor, acidic waters of the Okefenokee slow the decomposition of organic matter leading to an immense build-up of peat (partially decayed plant matter). In some places the peat is 15 feet deep. Should you need to exit your canoe or kayak in the middle of the swamp, do so very carefully. What appears to be solid ground may be a quagmire of soupy peat. The very name "Okefenokee" is an approximation of the Creek words for trembling earth. Use your paddle to test the ground before venturing and carry it with you as you go. Use it like a walking stick to aid in balance and also to distribute your weight over a greater area. Take small steps and transfer your weight gradually from one foot to the other. It is often best to avoid stepping in the same place twice. Once walked on, the structure of the peat is weakened, making it less stable the second time.

If you find yourself caught in a big, soupy hole with no firm footing, stay low, spread your body weight out as much as possible (this may mean crawling), use the paddle as a brace, and work your way to a clump of shrubs. The roots of the shrubs will offer firmer footing. Be especially careful in Durdin Prairie, where much of the peat is floating and very unstable.

Poisonous snakes. Any poisonous snake is potentially dangerous and should be treated with extreme caution, but they generally pose less of a threat than popular depictions would suggest. Usually they are just as interested in avoiding you as you are of avoiding them. Probably the greatest danger comes from surprising one at close quarters. Without an avenue of escape, the snake may strike to defend itself. The best preventive measure is to keep an eye out and watch where you place your hands and feet. Never approach, handle, harass, or otherwise disturb a poisonous snake; by doing so, you invite disaster. Also, please do not kill any poisonous snake. Not only are they remarkable animals and an integral part of the ecosystem, they are protected by refuge regulations.

Five different poisonous snakes occur in the Okefenokee: Florida Cottonmouth (Water Moccasin), Eastern Diamondback Rattlesnake, Canebrake (Timber) Rattlesnake, Dusky Pygmy Rattlesnake, and Eastern Coral Snake. Of these species, the one most likely to be encountered by canoeists is the Florida Cottonmouth. They spend much of their time along water margins hunting fish, frogs, and other animals. Their relative nonchalance in regard to humans has given them a misplaced reputation for aggressiveness. Rather than being aggressive, they just sort of hold their ground. Sometimes they even approach people in what seems like curiosity. This means that if you see one, you should give it a wide berth.

You are unlikely to encounter any of the rattlesnakes or the Eastern Coral Snake while canoeing in the Okefenokee. The magnificent Eastern Diamondback Rattlesnake, which can reach lengths of 6 feet or more, prefers the pine and palmetto uplands. The Canebrake and Dusky Pygmy Rattlesnakes inhabit the lowlands around the swamp border. If you see one, it will most likely be while you are loading or unloading at a launch site. The Canebrake is a large, beautiful snake, often richly colored. The Dusky Pygmy, as its name suggests, is a small (less than 2 feet long), well-camouflaged snake, easy to overlook. Eastern Coral Snakes are poisonous even though they lack the long fangs of the cottonmouth and rattlesnakes. They are found in a variety of habitats, but avoid the watery areas of the swamp interior. Their bright colors make them relatively easy to spot.

In the unlikely event that someone in your party is bitten by a poisonous snake, seek professional medical attention as quickly as possible. In the interim, remain calm and immobilize the area of the bite. Wash it with clean water, but do not apply tourniquets, cold water, or ice packs. Do not attempt to capture or kill the snake, since you will only increase the chance of further injury. In the case of a rattlesnake or cottonmouth bite, be sure to remove any restrictive jewelry or clothing from the affected limb.

Be aware that if you are canoeing in the middle of the swamp, it could be some time before you can get to a medical facility. This brings up the subject of the snakebite kit. Over the years snakebite advice has vacillated between recommending and discouraging the use of snakebite kits. The major concern is that improper use of the kit can cause more harm than good. Overly tight constriction bands restrict blood flow, and improper cuts lead to excessive bleeding or other injury. Another problem is using the kit when unnecessary, as in the case of dry strikes (no venom is passed) or when the snake turns out to be nonpoisonous.

Dr. Forgey, in *Wilderness Medicine*, recommends a device called the Extractor, manufactured by Sawyer. It is a safer and probably more effective alternative to the traditional, cut-and-suck snakebite kit, though its effectiveness has yet to be demonstrated convincingly in the field. It has the added advantage of being useful in other first-aid applications. The vacuum tube draws venom or debris out of a wound without the need for incisions or constriction bands.

We have only skimmed the basics of snakebite first-aid. This is one of those topics that you really need to get the latest and best advice from more detailed sources, preferably several.

Strong winds. Strong winds blow across the Okefenokee in association with storm systems and thunderstorms. The winds can make paddling difficult and strenuous, especially across the exposed sections of trail typical of the open prairies. Strong winds associated with thunderstorms can often be waited out in the protected lee of a patch of shrubs. Prolonged winds may simply have to be paddled through with grit and determination.

Thunderstorms and lightning. Thunderstorms are common afternoon and evening occurrences from May through September. They often begin as early as 2 P.M. and roll on well into the night. They can be very powerful and host a great deal of lightning. It is amazing how cold the rain can feel even when the air is so hot. The best way to avoid them is with an early start. Even so, you may get caught. Good preparation (rain gear for yourself and waterproof containers or bags for your equipment) will help fend off any inconvenience, but not the danger from lightning. During a thunderstorm seek cover, avoid tall isolated objects, remain low, and try not to be the tallest object in the area.

If the lightning danger is immediate, you should minimize your contact with conductive materials. This may require leaving your aluminum canoe. The problem is that you will likely be surrounded by swamp water, which is also highly conductive. If you can make it to an area of woods or shrubs, you may be able to exit your canoe and clamber onto the base of a tree or shrub above the water. Just remember not to pick an isolated group of trees, a lone tree, or the tallest tree in the vicinity. Always be extremely careful of peat quagmires when leaving your canoe. If you are not able to get out of your canoe safely, use the alpine hiker's technique of squatting on the balls of your feet with an insulative material (like a foam sleeping pad) between you and the canoe. Lightning victims should be given cardiopulmonary resuscitation as necessary and taken to medical facility as soon as possible.

3. Equipment

You don't need a lot of specialized equipment to paddle the Okefenokee. If you have a basic set of paddling and camping gear you probably have most of what you'll need. In addition to providing checklists, we have included equipment recommendations and a brief discussion of waterproof packing methods.

EQUIPMENT RECOMMENDATIONS

Watercraft. Virtually any stable, durable canoe is suitable for paddling in the Okefenokee: round-bottomed, flat-bottomed, solo, tandem, 16-foot, 17-foot, aluminum, wooden, fiberglass, Royalex, or Kevlar. Pick your favorite. Just keep in mind that long trips require a lot of paddling and a fair amount of gear. They will also take you through a variety of water and trail conditions. Canoes with large capacities, that have been designed for efficient paddling and wilderness tripping are often preferred.

Kayaks are also popular in the Okefenokee. (Touring designs are recommended.) Though we cannot speak from experience, it would seem that some narrow, twisting, peat-clogged sections of trail may be more difficult to navigate in a kayak than a canoe.

Inflatable watercraft are not recommended for use in the Okefenokee.

Paddles. For canoeing, our recommendation is a rugged paddle with a wide, square-tipped blade. If you prefer the efficiency of a bent shaft, consider carrying a standard, straight-shaft paddle as your backup for difficult sections of trail. Kayakers should consider two-section paddles, so that one half can be used to pole in constricted passages. Paddling gloves are highly recommended.

Tents. A free-standing design with insect netting is the best choice. Pitching a staked tent on the wooden platforms is a lesson in frustration. Suitable lash points are limited and inconvenient, making it difficult to secure even the fly lines of a free-standing tent. Bring plenty of extra rope in either case and be prepared to improvise. Small backpacking tents fit more easily in the limited spaces of the platforms, especially if several tents will be pitched. Of course if you will be limiting your camping to the islands, then either a free-standing backpacking tent or a staked cabin tent will work.

Cookstoves. Just a reminder that camp stoves are required for all cooking.

Portable toilets. A portable toilet with disposable bags is required on all overnight canoe trips. Since each overnight stop is outfitted with a composting toilet, this basically relegates the use of the portable toilet for waste generated en route. Don't feel obligated to use a commercial product. The requirement can be met with something as simple as a suitably sized tin can and a supply of plastic bags. A small amount of kitty litter added to the bags upon use will improve cleanliness and control odor.

CHECKLIST OF EQUIPMENT AND SUPPLIES

Routine use of a checklist will help you prepare for many safe and comfortable paddling trips. However, the particular gear and supplies that you pack for a given trip will depend on season, length of trip, whether you are a minimalist or comfort-craver, and many other factors. A good checklist, then, is a personal list that changes with circumstances and evolves over time.

The following lists include basic essentials and common equipment. A number of items that can add convenience or enjoyment are also included. Use the lists as a guide and modify them to suit your individual needs and tastes.

Basic supplies

- ❏ canoe or kayak
- ❏ tie rope, attached to bow
- ❏ paddles (including a spare)
- ❏ personal flotation device (required for each occupant of any boat)
- ❏ bailer and bailing sponge

- ❏ canoe permit and regulations (required on designated overnight canoe trips)
- ❏ map (required on designated overnight canoe trips)
- ❏ trail descriptions
- ❏ compass (required on designated overnight canoe trips)
- ❏ watch
- ❏ binoculars
- ❏ field identification guides
- ❏ pencil and paper for notes
- ❏ camera and film

- ❏ day pack or fanny pack
- ❏ waterproof packs/bags
- ❏ flashlight (required on designated overnight canoe trips)
- ❏ extra batteries and bulb
- ❏ extra flashlight
- ❏ weather radio
- ❏ dry matches (and more dry matches—placed in various dry pockets, compartments, etc.)

- ❏ waterproof fire starter
- ❏ lantern (especially for those short days in winter)
- ❏ first-aid kit (see below)
- ❏ survival kit (see below)
- ❏ repair kit (including sewing needles, thread, and safety pins)
- ❏ sunscreen
- ❏ lip balm
- ❏ insect repellent
- ❏ tent
- ❏ ground sheet
- ❏ extra rope
- ❏ sleeping bag
- ❏ sleeping pad
- ❏ duct tape

- ❏ water (general requirement is 1 gallon of drinking water per person per day, see page 8)
- ❏ water bottles
- ❏ food
- ❏ zip-locked bags
- ❏ paper towels
- ❏ cook kit (including cup, bowl, spoon, pot, pot holder, and can opener)
- ❏ pocket knife
- ❏ cook stove and fuel
- ❏ dish towel
- ❏ dish sponge

❏ biodegradable soap
❏ wash basin
❏ water purification backup (extra fuel, purification tablets, or water filter)
❏ garbage bags

❏ water shoes/sandals
❏ sneakers or boots
❏ broad-brimmed hat/cap
❏ sunglasses
❏ lightweight pants
❏ shorts
❏ long-sleeved shirt
❏ T-shirts
❏ underclothes
❏ socks (and extra socks)
❏ rainjacket and rainpants (or poncho)
❏ paddling or fingerless gloves
❏ sweatshirt
❏ insect headnet/suit

For cooler months add other layers, such as thermal underwear, wool sweater, jacket, warm hat, etc.

❏ portable toilet with disposable bags (required on designated overnight canoe trips)
❏ toilet paper
❏ personal toiletries
❏ hand towel
❏ face cloth
❏ book to read
❏ deck of cards

Basic first-aid kit
❏ pain reliever
❏ sunscreen
❏ antiseptic towelettes
❏ triple antibacterial ointment
❏ bandages (several varieties)
❏ gauze
❏ sterile wound closures
❏ sterile adhesive tape
❏ small scissors or knife

❏ moleskin
❏ CPR shield
❏ surgical gloves
❏ Sawyer Extractor
❏ first-aid instructions
❏ your normal medications

Optional first-aid items
❏ ace bandage
❏ triangle bandage
❏ inflatable splint
❏ salt tablets
❏ anti-diarrheal
❏ laxative
❏ antacid
❏ anaphylactic shock kit (for bee stings, insect bites)
❏ EMT sheers
❏ cotton swabs
❏ tweezers
❏ antihistamine such as Benadryl
❏ lip balm

Basic survival kit
❏ space blanket
❏ water purification tablets
❏ waterproof fire starter
❏ knife
❏ candle
❏ compass
❏ signal mirror
❏ whistle
❏ fishing line
❏ fish hooks (several sizes)
❏ lead sinkers

Optional survival items
❏ energy bars
❏ signal flares
❏ surgical tubing
❏ safety pins
❏ duct tape
❏ nylon rope

Consider a dry set of clothes, dry sleeping bag, and dry tent as part of your survival kit.

KEEPING YOUR GEAR DRY

Keeping your gear dry on a canoe trip is important, but can be a challenge. Take the time to develop a waterproof packing system before you hit the water. Bill Mason's *Song of the Paddle* contains an excellent discussion of different methods. Though few waterproofing methods are entirely reliable, you can expect many miles of worry-free paddling even with relatively simple techniques and inexpensive products.

Rugged, hard-sided, commercial waterproof containers are the safest choice. Highly resistant to puncture and usually waterproof when submerged, they are a particularly good choice for whitewater paddling, rough use, and valuable water-susceptible items such as cameras. Of course you will not have to worry about running any whitewater in the Okefenokee.

Soft-sided, commercial waterproof bags and packs also work well. Often constructed of PVC and featuring a roll-down closure, they will keep your gear dry under most conditions. Just keep in mind that they are less resistant to puncture than hard-sided containers and can leak if submerged.

If you do not have commercial products, you can use watertight, heavyweight plastic bags as waterproof pack liners (heavy-duty garbage bags will work in a pinch if you are careful with them). The trick is to protect the plastic bags from puncture and abrasion by sandwiching them between stuff sacks and packs. Begin by lining a suitable pack (heavy-duty rucksacks of the Duluth pack design work well) with one of the plastic bags. Make sure there is nothing inside the pack that could puncture or tear the plastic bag. If you are using garbage bags as liners, consider using a double layer for added durability and bring along a supply of spares to replace any that puncture or tear. Next, place your gear in unlined stuff sacks. Now put the gear-filled stuff sacks into the plastic bag in the pack. As with the pack, be careful of any protrusions or sharp objects that might tear the liner. Do not overfill the plastic bag; you want to be able to pull together at least 6 to 8 inches of loose bag at the top to fasten it. Twist the top of the plastic bag closed, fold it over onto itself, and secure it tightly with one or two rubber bands. Close the pack and you are ready to go.

Critical items, including a dry set of clothes, sleeping bags, and tents, should be doubly waterproofed; seal them in their own, individual waterproof bags before placing them in a waterproof pack. Soft items, such as clothes, sleeping bags, tent bodies, and flies, can often be placed directly into their regular stuff sacks lined with heavy duty garbage bags. If any of these items have sharp objects that could tear the liner, you will have to use two stuff sacks for each and sandwich the liner between them. In either case, stuff them as usual, then twist, fold, and secure the end of the garbage bag with a rubber band. Now they are ready to go into a waterproof pack. It is quick, easy, and inexpensive extra protection.

4. Calendar of Natural Events

January. Large numbers of birds overwinter throughout the swamp with Sandhill Cranes particularly abundant near the junction of Grand and Chesser prairies and in the vicinity of Gannet Lake. Waterfowl, such as Wood Ducks, Hooded Mergansers, and teal can be seen amid the prairies and backwaters. Tree Swallows and American Robins form large flocks, whereas Gray Catbirds disperse among the thickets.

February. The rites of spring arrive to the swamp as Ospreys begin nesting and Southern Leopard Frogs can be heard calling. Ferns raise new fiddleheads. Early blooming wildflowers, such as Neverwet, Arrowhead, and Climbing Heath, begin to flower.

March. Florida Cricket Frogs, Pig Frogs, and Carpenter Frogs join the choruses of Southern Leopard Frogs. Common Yellowthroats and Red-winged Blackbirds can be heard singing. Great Blue Herons and resident Sandhill Cranes begin nesting. More wildflowers begin to bloom as Hurrah Bush, Titi, Hatpins, bladderworts, and pawpaws open their blossoms. Pond Cypress begin to leaf out. Overwintering land birds and waterfowl depart. Alligators and aquatic turtles rouse from their winter lethargy and can be seen sunning on exposed banks and logs.

April. Land bird activity and variety increase as incoming migrants join residents. Swallow-tailed Kites, Red-headed Woodpeckers, Eastern Kingbirds,

An adult Black and Yellow Argiope spider on a stalk of yellow-eyed grass.

Chuck-will's-widows, Great Crested Flycatchers, Prothonotary Warblers, Yellow-throated Warblers, Northern Parulas, and others can be seen. Diligent searchers occasionally find the elusive Bachman's Sparrow in the Saw Palmetto uplands. Grass Pink, Fragrant Water Lily, Spatterdock, and Virginia Sweetspire are in bloom. Swallowtail butterflies visit the blossoms of wild irises, and the booming roar of bull alligators resonates across the swamp.

May. Many aquatic turtles are laying eggs. Wading birds become more conspicuous. Many land birds are in full song. Common Nighthawks perform aerial displays. Alligators are sunning less and becoming less visible as water temperatures rise. Pinewoods Treefrogs and Little Grass Frogs can be heard calling. Watershield, Arrow Arum, and pitcher plants are in bloom. Red-cockaded Woodpeckers are active at nesting colonies. Deer flies become active.

June. Many species of frog are calling as Southern Chorus Frogs and Green Treefrogs add their voices to evening sounds. Gopher Tortoises can be seen near their burrows in the late afternoon. Sweetbay Magnolia blooms.

July. Fully fledged wading birds leave the rookeries and begin foraging across the swamp. Wood Storks may be seen foraging in the prairies and along creek drainages if proper water levels are present. Loblolly Bay is in bloom. White-tailed Deer bucks grow their antlers. Wood Duck young are beginning to fly.

August. Wildlife is most active during the cooler hours of morning and evening. Blue-winged Teal arrive, signaling the beginning of the fall migration. Alligator young hatch out of their eggs and leave the nest.

September. Yellow-eyed grasses, Swamp Loosestrife, and other fall wildflowers are in bloom. Landbird migration includes Red-eyed Vireos, American Redstarts, Black-and-white Warblers, and Prairie Warblers.

October. Black Bears become more visible as they forage on the fall food crop. Land bird migration continues as Veeries pass through and Yellow-rumped Warblers and Hermit Thrushes arrive to spend the winter.

November. The close of the migration brings with it large numbers of Sandhill Cranes, Eastern Phoebes, Tree Swallows, and American Robins. Alligators become less active as water and air temperatures decline. Pond Cypress drop their needles.

December. Wading birds are prominent as they forage amid the prairies. Wood Ducks and teal can be seen throughout the swamp. Most overwintering birds have arrived. River Otters are more conspicuous in the lakes and prairies as alligators cease feeding.

5. Using This Guidebook

The trail descriptions include information on paddling conditions, scenery, mileages, wildlife, visitor use, and rest shelters. For your convenience the descriptions are divided into two chapters by type of trip: Overnight Trips and Day Trips. Because portions of some trails are open to both day tripping and overnight camping, they are described in each chapter. The Overnight Trips chapter is organized by trail. The Day Trips chapter is organized by access point.

The trail maps (see pages 121–131) were developed from a classified satellite image of the Okefenokee National Wildlife Refuge and digital versions of the 1994 series of United States Geological Survey (USGS) 1:24,000 quadrangle maps. Magnetic declination on the trail maps is between 3.5 and 4 degrees west. Guidebook nomenclature is based on the USGS maps. Supplemental information was added from a variety of sources, including refuge materials. To our knowledge, this is the first time that a classified satellite image has been used as the basis for the maps in an outdoor recreation guidebook. We hope that you like the results.

Distance. Determining exact distances and locations within the Okefenokee can be challenging. There are few prominent landmarks within the swamp's interior from which you can determine your position. For this book, all mileages between trail junctions were taken from digital versions of the 1994 series of United States Geological Survey (USGS) 1:24,000 maps and represent one-way distances. These include mileages listed on maps and those listed in the total distance heading of each trail section.

Mileage notations given throughout the trail narratives are derived from a variety of methods and are of varying accuracy. When possible, landmarks were used to determine positions and accurate distances were derived from USGS maps. In other instances, dead reckoning was used ("I reckon we've gone a mile"). In general, dead reckoning was used in conjunction with known positions and then adjusted as needed. Since these mileage notations refer only to general locations, they should prove adequate.

Be aware that mileage figures provided in this book were generated for the most part, independently of refuge mileage figures and the refuge's system of trail mile markers. Mileages provided in this book are not always in agreement with refuge figures.

Difficulty. The difficulty ratings provide a general assessment of the combined physical and technical demands of a particular section of trail. In practice, many trails exhibit a range of difficulty levels. The predominant difficulty level is listed.

When using the difficulty ratings, keep in mind that the flatwater paddling of the Okefenokee is often forgiving of imperfect paddling skills but less so of poor physical conditioning. Use mileage figures in conjunction with the difficulty ratings to assess the suitability of a particular route for your own skills and conditioning.

Twelve miles of easy paddling may prove difficult for a skilled, yet poorly conditioned, paddler.

Also remember that water levels profoundly affect the actual conditions that you may encounter. A pleasant paddle at high water may turn into an arduous pull-and-drag at low water. Most trails become more difficult to traverse as water levels drop. Ask refuge personnel about current conditions.

Easy: Wide, gently curving trails with little impeding vegetation and few obstacles. Command of basic paddling skills and moderate physical conditioning are recommended.

Moderate: Winding, narrow trails subject to wind, occasional obstacles, and impeding vegetation growing within the trail. Command of basic paddling skills, knowledge of a variety of strokes (draw, pry, brace, etc.), and good physical conditioning are recommended.

Difficult: Constricted, twisty trails often with obstacles, tight turns, overhanging trees and shrubs, impeding vegetation, and peat blow-ups (mats of floating peat). While navigating these trails, you may have to exit your craft in shallow water or on unstable ground and drag or pull it across obstacles. Command of basic paddling skills, experience with a variety of strokes, and good to very good physical conditioning are recommended.

Type of trail

The type of trail is listed to give you an idea of the paddling conditions that can be expected along a section of trail.

Canal: Large, straight or gently curving channels that are 25 to 60 feet wide, 5 to 7 feet deep, and mostly free of impeding vegetation and obstacles.

Boat trail: Small, winding or twisting trails that are typically 4 to 12 feet wide and 2 to 4 feet deep. These trails are susceptible to encroaching vegetation, constricted passages, and obstacles.

Natural channel: The natural river and creek channels of the Suwannee River drainage. Some are wide, deep, and gently curving. Others are narrow, shallow, and twisty. The smaller, creek-like channels are susceptible to drought, constricted passages, and obstacles. Currents are typically less than 2 miles per hour.

Hazards. Some prominent hazards are listed for each trail. These hazards are discussed in Chapter 2, "Hazards," page 14.

Habitats. Habitats are listed to provide a quick description of the type of scenery that the trail traverses. From the habitats you can also deduce the types of plants and wildlife that you are likely to encounter.

Prairie: Shallow marshes with an abundance of low-growing forbs. Two types of prairie can be distinguished: emergent and water lily. Emergent prairies are dominated by a variety of grasses, sedges, and leafy forbs. Common plants include Walter's Sedge, beakrushes, yellow-eyed grasses, Maidencane, Broomsedge, and Redroot. Water lily prairies occur in slightly deeper water and are dominated by long-stemmed and surface-floating plants, such as Fragrant Water Lily, Neverwet, bladderworts, and Arrowhead. A variety of frogs, wading birds, and waterfowl inhabit Okefenokee's prairies.

Shrubland: Shrubby thickets and low stands of scrubby trees. Often forming a transition zone between prairie and forest, Okefenokee's shrublands infiltrate nearly every opening with filigree-like fingers and sprawling patches. In some areas of the swamp the shrubs form extensive thickets. Common species include Hurrah Bush, Titi, Poor-man's Soap, Swamp Fetterbush, Virginia Sweetspire, and hollies. Many land birds inhabit Okefenokee's shrublands including Gray Catbirds, American Robins (winter), Carolina Wrens, and Common Yellowthroats.

Wooded Swamp: Mature forests of Pond Cypress, gums, bays, and Red Maple. Swampy woodlands are the Okefenokee's dominant feature, covering more than 50 percent of the swamp. Pond Cypress and bay forests are typical of the areas of stillwater in central and eastern portions of the swamp. Forests of Black Gum, Red Maple, and Pond Cypress occur along watercourses and throughout the Suwannee River drainage. Common birds of the Okefenokee's wooded swamps include Pileated Woodpeckers, Red-shouldered Hawks, Barred Owls, and Yellow-throated Warblers (summer).

Lake: Relatively small, open-water lakes. Most of the Okefenokee's lakes are likely the result of fire burning away the peaty substrate during drought and then the area later filling with water. Others, such as Billys Lake, lie over depressions in the underlying sand base of the swamp. Alligators, aquatic turtles, and a variety of waterfowl frequent Okefenokee's lakes.

Reliability. The reliability rating provides a gauge of the probability that a section of trail will be open and passable to canoe and kayak travel.

Poor: Trail subject to regular, sometimes annual, closings due to low water. These typically occur during late fall and early winter.

Moderate: Trail typically remains open and passable throughout most years.

Good: Trail is closed or becomes impassable only during severe drought.

USGS Maps. This section lists the United States Geological Survey (USGS) 7.5-minute quadrangle topographic maps that apply to each section of trail. They can be purchased from many outdoor recreation stores, some bookstores, or directly from the USGS office listed on the following page. Be aware that there are two series of USGS maps for the Okefenokee. The old 1965-1967 series is suppose to be out of circulation, but may still be on the shelf of your local store. The 1965-1967 maps are more detailed and easier to use, but do not properly depict the current paths of the trails (some trails are not even included). The 1994 series, though less detailed, has updated trail depictions.

Also be aware that the USGS produces a set of 30 x 60 minute quadrangle maps of the Okefenokee ("Okefenokee Swamp, GA-FL" and "Waycross, GA"). As with the 1965-1967 series, these maps do not depict current routes of the canoe trails.

U.S. Geological Survey
Box 25286
Denver, Colorado 80225
1-800-HELP-MAP
VISA or MasterCard orders can be faxed to 303-202-4693

Visitor use. Recreational use varies considerably within the refuge and is dependent upon the area and the use restrictions. Even on portions of trails limited to canoe parties with permits, you may encounter refuge staff and other officials or cross paths with other canoe parties. The visitor use rating provides a general assessment of the number of people likely to be encountered on a particular section of trail.

Light: Infrequent or rare encounters with other visitors.

Moderate: Regular encounters with other visitors.

Heavy: Frequent or continuous encounters with other visitors.

6. Refuge Access Points

There are four main access points to the canoe and boat trails of the Okefenokee National Wildlife Refuge: Suwannee Canal Recreation Area, Kingfisher Landing, Suuwannee River Sill Recreation Area, and Stephen C. Foster State Park. Each site is equipped with a parking lot and boat ramp. Other facilities, services, and recreational opportunities vary by location and are described separately for each site in the following listings.

EAST ENTRANCE: SUWANNEE CANAL RECREATION AREA

Refuge Headquarters:
U.S. Fish and Wildlife Service
Okefenokee National Wildlife Refuge
Route 2 Box 3330
Folkston, GA 31537
912-496-7366

Concessionaire:
Suwannee Canal Recreation Concession, Inc.
Route 2 Box 3325
Folkston, GA 31537
912-496-7156

General location: 8 miles south of Folkston, Georgia.
Permits and fees: Fee required at entrance and for boat ramp use. Permit and fee required for overnight canoe and kayak trips. Paddlers with valid overnight canoe permits are not required to pay the entrance fee.
Activities: Day-use canoeing and kayaking, overnight canoe and kayak trips, motorboating, guided tours, wildlife observation, fishing, and hiking.
Hours of operation: The entrance gate, restrooms, picnic area, boat ramp, and store are open between 8 A.M. and 6 P.M. from September 11 through February 28, and between 7 A.M. and 7:30 P.M. from March 1 through September 10. The visitor center is open daily between 9 A.M. and 4 P.M. from September 11 through February 28, and between 9 A.M. and 5 P.M. from March 1 through September 10. The refuge headquarters is open weekdays between 7 A.M. and 3:30 P.M.
Visitor use: Moderate to heavy.

Overview: The Suwannee Canal Recreation Area contains the refuge headquarters, visitor center, restrooms, picnic area, boat basin, public boat ramp, and privately operated concessionaire. There is also a wildlife drive, which leads to a couple of foot trails, a restored homestead, and a 4,000-foot boardwalk with observation tower. The visitor center is modern and has several nice exhibits. The concessionaire operates a shuttle service and rents canoes, paddles, personal flotation devices, and a variety of camping equipment. There are no camping facilities or other overnight accommodations available. (See "Nearby Accommodations and Services," page 144, for services located outside of the refuge.) The Suwannee Canal Recreation Area is the most heavily visited area of the swamp. Even on the busiest of days, however, the crowds thin considerably beyond the first several miles from the boat basin. Overall, visitor use ranges from moderate to heavy.

Finding the launch area: From Folkston, Georgia, travel 8 miles south on Georgia 121/23 to the entrance sign. Turn right onto Georgia 121 Spur and continue west for 4 miles to the parking lot at the end of the road.

NORTHEAST ENTRANCE: KINGFISHER LANDING

General location: 14 miles northwest of Folkston, Georgia.
Permits and fees: No entrance or boat ramp fees. Permit and fee required for overnight canoe and kayak trips.
Activities: Day-use canoeing and kayaking, overnight canoe and kayak trips, motorboating, wildlife observation, and fishing.
Hours of operation: 5:30 A.M. to 7:30 P.M. from September 11 through February 28, and 5:30 A.M. to 9 P.M. from March 1 through September 10.
Visitor use: Light to moderate.

Overview: Kingfisher Landing provides access to the canals and boat trails of the northeastern portion of the refuge. It is an access point only, and few facilities are provided. There is a parking lot and public boat ramp. The refuge usually maintains a composting toilet at the landing. Kingfisher Landing is the least used access point. Visitor use is typically light.

Finding the launch area: From Folkston, Georgia follow U.S. Highway 1 north for 12 miles from its junction with Main Street to Kingfisher Landing Road (an unmarked dirt road). Turn left (west), crossing the railroad tracks, onto Kingfisher Landing Road and continue 1.6 miles to the parking lot. This road can be a little tricky to find, so watch carefully for the "Kingfisher Landing" sign marking the turn. There is also a large "Race Pond" sign along the eastern side of the road at the junction. Kingfisher Landing Road can also be reached from Waycross, Georgia by following U.S. Highway 1 south for 20 miles.

WEST ENTRANCE

Suwannee River Sill Recreation Area

General location: 12 miles northeast of Fargo, Georgia.
Permits and fees: No entrance or boat ramp fees. Permit required only if crossing Suwannee River Sill with boat.
Activities: Day-use canoeing and kayaking, motorboating, wildlife observation, fishing, and hiking.
Hours of Operation: 7 A.M. to 7 P.M. from mid-September through February 28,

and 6:30 A.M. to 8:30 P.M. from March 1 through mid-September.
Visitor use: Moderate.

Overview: The Suwannee River Sill Recreation Area has a boat ramp, parking lot, and foot trails. It is a day-use access point only. Camping or other services are not available. It is a favorite spot of local anglers, and the number of people you are likely to encounter is almost directly proportional to the quality of fishing at the time. Typically, the area receives only moderate use.

Finding the launch area: From Fargo, Georgia travel 1 mile south on Georgia 94 to Georgia 177. Turn left onto Georgia 177 and continue 10.5 miles to the refuge entrance. Shortly past the entrance gate, turn left onto the paved road and follow it to the parking lot.

Stephen C. Foster State Park
Stephen C. Foster State Park:
Route 1 Box 131
Fargo, GA 31631
912-637-5274

General location: 17 miles northeast of Fargo, Georgia.
Permits and fees: Fee required at entrance and for boat ramp use. Permit and fee required for overnight canoe and kayak trips. Paddlers with valid overnight canoe trip permits are not required to pay the entrance fee.
Activities: Day-use canoeing and kayaking, overnight canoe and kayak trips, motorboating, guided tours, wildlife observation, and fishing.
Hours of operation: 7 A.M. to 7 P.M. from mid-September through February 28, and 6:30 A.M. to 8:30 P.M. from March 1 through mid-September. The park office is open 8 A.M. to 5 P.M. from mid-September through February 28, and 7 A.M. to 6 P.M. from March 1 through mid-September.
Visitor use: Moderate to heavy.

Overview: Stephen C. Foster State Park is operated by the Georgia Department of Natural Resources in cooperation with the Okefenokee National Wildlife Refuge. The park is fully equipped with interpretive center, museum, picnic area, restrooms, campground, cottages, dumping station, canoe rental, store, boat basin, and public boat ramp. Stephen C. Foster State Park is another well-used access point. Convenient access to Billys Lake and the Suwannee River make the area popular with campers, anglers, and paddlers alike. However, as with the Suwannee Canal Recreation Area, the number of people you are likely to encounter diminishes quickly a few miles beyond the boat basin. Visitor use is typically moderate.

Finding the launch area: From Fargo, Georgia travel 1 mile south on Georgia 94 to Georgia 177. Turn left onto Georgia 177 and continue 17 miles to the parking lot.

7. Overnight Trips

Canoe and kayak camping trips within the Okefenokee National Wildlife Refuge are administered through the refuge's system of designated overnight canoe trips. Twelve different trips are available by reservation and permit (see "Designated Overnight Canoe Trips and Mileage Chart," pages 37 and 38, and "Permits," page 12). Each campsite is limited to a single party per night. The trips range in length from two to five days and offer a variety of scenery and paddling conditions.

Some of the overnight trips start and end at the same location (loops and out-and-backs). Others start and end at different locations (shuttles) and require special transportation arrangements. If two vehicles are available, you can park one at the take-out before starting the trip. (Each vehicle must display a parking placard issued by the refuge.) Allow plenty of time for shuttling and make sure that you have keys and proper tie-down equipment when you arrive at the take-out; it is 95 miles from Kingfisher Landing to Stephen C. Foster State Park. A commercial shuttle service is available through the Suwannee Canal Recreation Concession, Inc. (see "East Entrance," page 33).

The refuge's 12 designated overnight canoe trips utilize only six different trails (Red, Green, Blue, Purple, Orange, and Brown), so a particular trip may follow all or only a portion of one or more trails. For ease of use, our trail descriptions divide each of the trails into segments between important trail junctions and overnight stops. The chart on pages 37 and 38 allows you to follow the refuge's designated trips using the trail descriptions in this book. Simply find the trip you are interested in and, for each day or leg of that trip, read across the chart to the right. In the second column, you will find one or more numbers in black boxes—these are the numbers of the trip descriptions in *Paddling Okefenokee*. To read the narrative of that trip/trail section, turn to the appropriate numbered description(s) in the pages that follow. Note that some descriptions will need to be followed in the reverse of their written order; the trip numbers for these instances are accompanied by an "r" in the chart. The third column of the chart gives the mileage for each leg.

For instance, the refuge's designated canoe trip number 5 (Kingfisher Landing–Bluff Lake–Floyds Island–Stephen C. Foster State Park) starts at Kingfisher Landing and follows the Green Trail to the first night's campsite at Bluff Lake shelter (our Trip 6). From the Bluff Lake shelter, the trip continues along the Green Trail to Floyds Island, the second night's campsite (our trips 7 and 8). After the short portage across Floyds Island, the trip follows the Green Trail to the junction with the Red Trail, then follows the Red Trail south to Stephen C. Foster State Park (our trips 9, 10, and 5, in that order).

Designated Overnight Canoe Trips and Mileage Chart

Description of Officially Designated Trip	Our Trip Number*	Distance
DESIGNATED OVERNIGHT TRIP NO. 1		
Day 1: Kingfisher Landing to Bluff Lake	`6`	7.6 miles
Day 2: Bluff Lake to Kingfisher Landing	`6r`	7.6 miles
DESIGNATED OVERNIGHT TRIP NO. 2 *(From Suwannee Canal Recreation Area)*		
Day 1: Suwannee Canal Recreation Area to Canal Run	`15` `16`	9.9 miles
or		
Stephen C. Foster State Park to Canal Run	`17r`	7.6 miles
Day 2: Canal Run to Suwannee Canal Recreation Area	`16r` `15r`	9.9 miles
or		
Canal Run to Stephen C. Foster State Park	`17`	7.6 miles
DESIGNATED OVERNIGHT TRIP NO. 3		
Day 1: Stephen C. Foster State Park to Cravens Hammock	`18`	11.2 miles
Day 2: Cravens Hammock to Stephen C. Foster State Park	`18r`	11.2 miles
DESIGNATED OVERNIGHT TRIP NO. 4		
Day 1: Kingfisher Landing to Maul Hammock	`1`	12.2 miles
Day 2: Maul Hammock to Big Water	`2`	12 miles
Day 3: Big Water to Stephen C. Foster State Park	`4` `5`	7.8 miles
DESIGNATED OVERNIGHT TRIP NO. 5		
Day 1: Kingfisher Landing to Bluff Lake	`6`	7.6 miles
Day 2: Bluff Lake to Floyds Island	`7` `8`	8.6 miles
Day 3: Floyds Island to Stephen C. Foster State Park	`9` `10` `5`	8.8 miles
DESIGNATED OVERNIGHT TRIP NO. 6		
Day 1: Kingfisher Landing to Bluff Lake	`6`	7.6 miles
Day 2: Bluff Lake to Round Top	`7` `11` `14r`	11.2 miles
Day 3: Round Top to Suwannee Canal Recreation Area	`13r` `15r`	11.4 miles
DESIGNATED OVERNIGHT TRIP NO. 7		
Day 1: Suwannee Canal Recreation Area to Round Top	`15` `13`	11.4 miles
Day 2: Round Top to Floyds Island	`14` `11r` `8`	4.6 miles
Day 3: Floyds Island to Suwannee Canal Recreation Area	`8r` `11` `12` `16r` `15r`	13.3 miles
or		
Floyds Island to Stephen C. Foster State Park	`9` `10` `15`	8.8 miles
DESIGNATED OVERNIGHT TRIP NO. 8		
Day 1: Stephen C. Foster State Park to Floyds Island	`5r` `10r` `9r`	8.8 miles
Day 2: Floyds Island to Canal Run	`8r` `11` `12`	3.8 miles
Day 3: Canal Run to Stephen C. Foster State Park	`17`	7.6 miles

* An *r* (e.g. `12r`) following the trip number in this column indicates that the trip must be done in the reverse of its presentation in this book.

Description of Officially Designated Trip	Our Trip Number	Distance
DESIGNATED OVERNIGHT TRIP NO. 9		
Day 1: Kingfisher Landing to Bluff Lake	**6**	7.6 miles
Day 2: Bluff Lake to Floyds Island	**7** **8**	8.6 miles
Day 3: Floyds Island to Canal Run	**8r** **11** **12**	3.8 miles
Day 4: Canal Run to Stephen C. Foster State Park	**17**	7.6 miles
or		
Canal Run to Suwannee Canal Recreation Area	**16r** **15r**	9.9 miles
DESIGNATED OVERNIGHT TRIP NO. 10		
Day 1: Kingfisher Landing to Bluff Lake	**6**	7.6 miles
Day 2: Bluff Lake to Floyds Island	**7** **8**	8.6 miles
Day 3: Floyds Island to Round Top	**8r** **11** **14r**	4.6 miles
Day 4: Round Top to Suwannee Canal Recreation Area	**13r** **15r**	11.4 miles
DESIGNATED OVERNIGHT TRIP NO. 11		
Day 1: Kingfisher Landing to Maul Hammock	**1**	12.2 miles
Day 2: Maul Hammock to Big Water	**2**	12 miles
Day 3: Big Water to Floyds Island	**3** **9r**	3.8 miles
Day 4: Floyds Island to Bluff Lake	**8r** **7r**	8.6 miles
DESIGNATED OVERNIGHT TRIP NO. 12		
Day 1: Kingfisher Landing to Maul Hammock	**1**	12.2 miles
Day 2: Maul Hammock to Big Water	**2**	12 miles
Day 3: Big Water to Floyds Island	**3** **9r**	3.8 miles
Day 4: Floyds Island to Canal Run	**8r** **11** **12**	3.8 miles
Day 5: Canal Run to Stephen C. Foster State Park	**17**	7.6 miles
or		
Canal Run to Suwannee Canal Recreation Area	**16r** **15r**	9.9 miles

RED TRAIL

1 Kingfisher Landing to Maul Hammock Shelter

Distance: 12.2 miles. See map on page 122
Difficulty: Moderate to difficult.
Type of trail: Canal, boat trail.
Hazards: Peat quagmires, lightning, heat exhaustion, motorboats, airboats, biting insects.
Habitats: Shrubland, wooded swamp, lake.
Reliability: Good.
USGS maps: Double Lakes-GA, Fort Mudge-GA, Waycross SE-GA.
Visitor use: Light to moderate; portions open to day-use boating.

Overview: This section of trail is one of the longest in the swamp. Get an early start, especially during the shorter days of winter. Starting in the canal at Kingfisher Landing on the northeastern side of the swamp, the trail travels north and west to the overnight shelter on the wonderfully sublime Maul Hammock Lake. It is an intimate trail, meandering through a mix of dense shrublands and young woods. Along the way small patches of prairie and a number of small lakes provide varied scenery. Wood Ducks regularly feed along the trail, and quiet canoeists may surprise them around any bend. Watch for Great Egrets and Sandhill Cranes in the prairies, and Gray Catbirds amidst the extensive shrubs. On the lakes you may see Blue-winged and Green-winged Teal (winter), Pied-billed Grebes (winter), and Anhingas. Alligators are present, but you are not likely to see them. In the fall, spiders build a procession of webs across the trail; passing through the innumerable silken strands can be either exhilarating or exasperating, depending on the degree of your penchant for spiders.

Despite being open to day-use boating to mile 5.1, this trail is still one of your best opportunities to find some wilderness solitude in the Okefenokee. Just remember that the length of the trail and it's winding path can make for slow and tiring paddling. Water levels are usually sufficient for paddling, and the trail only rarely closes due to drought.

The trail: The put-in is at Kingfisher Landing, the same one used for the Green Trail. The two trails follow a common path for the first mile down the canal. There is a parking lot and boat ramp but few other facilities. Make certain that you have everything you need for your trip before you arrive—including water. At times the refuge maintains a composting toilet at the landing.

The first 5.1 miles of the trail are open to day-use boating, so you may encounter motorboat operators, kayakers, and canoeists at the ramp, in the canals, and on the trail as far as Double Lakes. (Special permits are occasionally provided for motorboat use to Maul Hammock Lake.) However, this area is much less used than either Stephen C. Foster State Park or Suwannee Canal Recreation Area, and it is unlikely that you will encounter anyone beyond the canal (mile 1.6).

Maul Hammock Lake.

The trail begins in the 40- to 50-foot-wide canal, a product of peat dredging operations that were based at the landing in the 1950s. The roomy, open waters of the canal not only allow for enchanting reflections, they also give you the chance to polish up your paddling strokes or get in sync with your partner. (You know the drill, "Port draw, port draw, port draw. Oops, I mean the other side.") Tall Slash Pine, Loblolly Bay, and Dahoon Holly line the embankments. Numerous shrubs—Titi, Swamp Fetterbush, Wax Myrtle, and Hurrah Bush—vie for space under the trees, and in a few places Maidencane and yellow-eyed grasses find a niche.

After about 1 mile you pass the Green Trail/Bluff Lake turnoff on the southern side of the canal. Continue northwest, following the markers for the Red Trail and Maul Hammock. In about 0.3 mile a wide band of Spatterdock forms along the southwestern margin of the canal. If you nose quietly along its edge, you may spot a frog or two before they dive out of sight. Announcing their alarm (or mockery) many of the Southern Leopard Frogs emit a funny, little *"ereep"* as they leap to safety. In summer Green Herons nest in the thick shrubbery along the trail. And of course, anywhere you find deep water in the Okefenokee, you may also find an alligator.

Very near the end of the canal (mile 1.6) the trail jogs off to the west and becomes a winding, 5- to 10-foot-wide boat trail. Cypress stands and scattered pines intermingle with patches of shrubs and emergent prairie. A few pockets of water lily prairie dot the way. The jumbled mix is the kind of place that Common Yellowthroats love. Their *"witchity, witchity, witchity"* songs and *"chet"* calls are as much a fixture of the landscape as the cypress.

At mile 1.8 a spur trail leaves from the northeastern side and leads to little Trout Lake. Though this 0.5-mile spur eventually rejoins the Red Trail at mile 2.2, the last portions are overgrown and difficult to paddle. You are probably better off keeping to the left (west) and staying on the main path of the Red Trail.

Between mile 2 and mile 3, shrubs become more prevalent and the isolated cypress stands coalesce, eventually forming rambling woodlands. Openings in the forest are occupied by sedge runs and water lily pools. Watch for a variety of woodpeckers (Pileated, Red-bellied, and Northern Flicker), chattering and cackling in the trees. Northern Mockingbirds and Eastern Phoebes (winter) often sit atop conspicuous perches to keep a lookout for passing insects and approaching foes.

Past mile 3 the trail continues through the broken cypress forest. The old, moss-covered stands with their widely spaced trunks grow over a well-developed understory of Titi and Hurrah Bush. In contrast, the young, dense stands crowd together in tight masses, barely leaving room for a few grasses.

Approaching mile 4, low shrubs restrict the vista to little more than the trail and occasional glimpses into brushy openings. Isolated cypress stands, scattered pine, and a few Loblolly Bay comprise the remnants of the dwindling forest. The secure cover of the thick tangle attracts a contingent of Gray Catbirds, Common Yellowthroats, Swamp Sparrows (winter), and Northern Mockingbirds.

Much of the Okefenokee is covered by shrubs—nearly 30 percent. While the shrublands don't provide scenic views of broad vistas, the sheltered, shady environs are a good place to study some of the Okefenokee's intricate details, such as the diversity of lichens encrusting the trees or the variety of the shrubs themselves. Hurrah Bush is the robust shrub with thick, dark green leaves. Typically broad and roughly oval, Hurrah Bush leaves often end with a pointed tip. Titi leaves are much slimmer and a lighter shade of green. They have a characteristic reverse taper (the leaves are slimmest toward the base). Titi can also be recognized by the dried, beadlike fruit clusters that dangle from its twigs long after it has finished flowering. Swamp Fetterbush is a delicate, slender-branched shrub. It has slim, papery leaves with fine teeth all along the margin. Poor-man's Soap also has papery leaves, but they are broader and have teeth only on the distal margin (the half toward the leaf tip).

Near mile 4.5 the shrubs begin to thin and mix with young cypress, pine, and clumps of Plume Grass. Then the shrubs retreat, and an emergent prairie of yellow-eyed grasses and sedges fills the opening. Great Egrets, Little Blue Herons, and White Ibis can regularly be seen wading in the water lily pools in search of Florida Cricket Frogs and sunfishes.

At mile 4.9 a short spur trail forks off to the left (west-southwest) and leads 0.2 mile to the first lake in this set of Double Lakes. (The Okefenokee has two sets of Double Lakes; the other set is located in Grand Prairie.) The 17-acre lake makes for a nice diversion, but it is not particularly scenic or rich with wildlife. A few alligators, Anhingas, and teal (winter) make their home on it, and numerous frogs populate the Spatterdock-covered margins; otherwise, the lake is usually quiet. If you decide to make the extra excursion to explore the lake, be sure that you have sufficient time and strength to make it the rest of the way to Maul Hammock.

The main trail bypasses the lake and follows an arm of Carters Prairie extending north. During the warm months, dragonflies patrol the area like squadrons of miniature fighter planes, zipping, swooping, and barnstorming in all directions. Consider yourself lucky if one opts to use the top of your head as a temporary look out since such a companion is great for warding off the deer flies in May and June.

Just past Double Lakes, near mile 5.1, you reach the sign that marks the limit of day-use boating. In addition to refuge staff, cooperating officials, and canoe trip parties, a few anglers are issued special permits and allowed to take motorboats past this point as far as Maul Hammock Lake for the day. In all likelihood though, you will be surrounded by wonderful solitude for the rest of the way to Maul Hammock.

As you continue, the shrubs thicken—fringing the cypress stands and pervading the surrounding prairie. In winter you often see large flocks of Tree Swallows. Sometimes they simply pass silently overhead; other times they skim low over the water and catch the rising insects out of midair. Once in a while, on certain cold mornings when the sun is shining but has yet to warm the air enough for insects to take flight, a flock will descend on some bare sapling standing full to the sun. They roost gathered tightly together, fluttering about to find a perch, and virtually cover the sapling.

At mile 6.1 you cross Pond Lake, a small lake covered with Fragrant Water Lily and Spatterdock. From Pond Lake to Christmas Lake at mile 6.9, you paddle through dispersed shrublands and patches of sedges, Maidencane, and Redroot. Barred Owls, Pileated Woodpeckers, Wood Ducks, and Belted Kingfishers are among the birds you might find. The area often harbors rails (a secretive marsh bird), which are a rare sight in the Okefenokee. Christmas Lake, though not much larger than Pond Lake, holds some open water.

Past Christmas Lake the trail plunges into shrubs and forest. Titi, Hurrah Bush, and Poor-man's Soap form a shaded corridor with Loblolly Bay, Slash Pine, and Pond Cypress in the overstory. Overhanging branches and vines occasionally reach out across the trail, but generally cause little hindrance.

An abrupt break in the shrubs at mile 7.8 places you at the edge of Ohio Lake. Spatterdock finds root across much of this 0.3-mile-long lake, but the trail passes through the mostly open water of its center. Check the marshy edges for Anhingas, Blue-winged and Green-winged Teals (winter), Wood Ducks, and Pied-billed Grebes (winter). The lake is not quite large enough for the birds to feel secure sharing it with you, and any that you find will probably take flight before you finish crossing.

Past Ohio Lake the shrub corridor continues, and for the next 2.5 miles the trail weaves through a profuse expanse of boggy shrubland. A dense thicket of

The overnight shelter at Maul Hammock Lake.

Titi, Hurrah Bush, and bamboo vine borders the trail, creating a wall of shrubs that becomes a veritable tunnel at times. A few Loblolly Bays, Pond Cypresses, and Slash Pines infiltrate the thicket in small copses or as lone stragglers.

Approaching mile 11 the shrub corridor begins to break up, making room for a few shrubby clearings and small wet-meadows. Before long the thick shrubs give way to scattered thickets, disjointed woodlands, and prairie openings. A variety of birds can be found in the heterogeneous landscape. Watch for Common Yellowthroats, Yellow-rumped Warblers (winter), and Swamp Sparrows (winter) in the shrubby tangles; Great Egrets and White Ibis in the flooded prairies; and Red-shouldered Hawks and Pileated Woodpeckers in the skies as they rove from woodland to woodland.

At mile 12.2 take the short spur trail to the left (west), which leads to Maul Hammock Lake and the overnight shelter. The shelter sits against the woods on the northern edge of the lake and has a nice view.

The lake, though not particularly large, consists mostly of open water surrounded by a shrubby border. At dusk and dawn it reflects the muted colors of twilight's serene beauty. Alligators are present, and a few Pig Frogs grunt the nights away during spring and summer. The shelter is in good condition and is a popular roost for the local vultures.

As with most of the shelters, when the wind drops off in the evening, the ventilating turbine on the roof of the toilet stops spinning. Wise campers will use the facility early. Unfortunately, mornings are also usually calm, and you will probably want to use it and be on your way before the breeze picks up.

Also be forewarned that the Raccoons of Maul Hammock can be persistent prowlers. Hang your gear well, so you don't have to go on patrol every time you hear their approaching footsteps.

2 Maul Hammock Shelter to Big Water Shelter

Distance: 12 miles.

See map on page 123

Difficulty: Moderate to difficult.
Type of trail: Boat trail, natural channel.
Hazards: Peat quagmires, lightning, heat exhaustion, motorboats, constricted passages, airboats, alligators, biting insects.
Habitats: Prairie, wooded swamp, lake.
Reliability: Moderate.
USGS maps: Dinner Pond-GA, Waycross SE-GA.
Visitor use: Light to moderate; portions open to day-use boating.

Overview: Beginning at the Maul Hammock overnight shelter, this 12-mile section of trail travels west and south through Sapling Prairie into the upper reaches of that famous southern river, the Suwannee. It is an interesting and varied section of trail, taking you from a mosaic of prairie and cypress into a large wooded forest, and finally to the lazy, cypress-bordered sections of the Suwannee River.

The Big Water overnight shelter sits 0.1 mile east of the river along the Red Trail Spur. Great Egrets, White Ibis, and Wood Ducks are the most common species encountered, though Sandhill Cranes, Great Blue Herons, Red-shouldered Hawks, Belted Kingfishers, and Eastern Phoebes (winter) also frequent the area. Numerous frogs can be seen or heard calling, especially during the spring. In April, swallowtail butterflies feed on the nectar of wild irises along the trail. Day-use access is permitted from Stephen C. Foster State Park to Big Water Lake, though this deep into the swamp it is unlikely that you will meet anyone on the trail. As part of the upper drainage of the Middle Fork of the Suwannee River, portions of the trail are susceptible to drought and can become difficult to traverse during periods of low water. Get an early start and be prepared for a fairly long, slow paddle.

The trail: From the Maul Hammock overnight shelter follow the left fork of the spur trail back out to the main path of the Red Trail, then head northwest (left again) through Sapling Prairie. The winding boat trail is 5 to 10 feet wide and typically 2 to 3 feet deep. Fragrant Water Lily, yellow-eyed grasses, and sedges rim the channel, but the center of the trail stays relatively free of vegetation and offers pleasant paddling.

The surrounding cypress forest covers the land like a half-finished jigsaw puzzle—partially connected and rife with holes. Low thickets and prairie meadows occupy the innumerable gaps. Walter's Sedge, yellow-eyed grasses, Titi,

Hurrah Bush, and Swamp Fetterbush predominate, but clumps of Maidencane, Broomsedge, and Hooded Pitcher Plant are sprinkled about as well.

Sapling Prairie reveals itself in stages. Winding fingers, nestled pockets, and broken expanses of prairie lie irregularly amid the patchy forest.

Keep an eye out for Wood Ducks, Common Yellowthroats, Red-shouldered Hawks, Eastern Phoebes (winter), and the Black and Turkey Vultures that teeter and glide overhead. Though the numerous frogs are more difficult to spy, you can still enjoy their seasonal choruses. Listen for the harsh clicking of Florida Cricket Frogs, the echoed knocking of Carpenter Frogs, and the low grunting of Pig Frogs.

Past mile 13, the trail winds through a blend of forest and prairie. Then the airy mix constricts, and you pass through a couple of short wooded corridors. From there the trail enters spacious tracts of broken prairie. Sedges, Maidencane, Neverwet, and Fragrant Water Lily are interspersed with small, Titi shrub-islands and cypress domes (the dome-shaped stands of Pond Cypress).

At mile 14.3 the trail makes a sharp bend to the left where an unmaintained boat trail enters from the northwest. Stay to the left (southeast) and continue along the Red Trail.

The prairie vistas provide excellent wildlife viewing. Great Egrets and Little Blue Herons often forage along the edges of the water lily pools. Sandhill Cranes, standoffish and wary, are most likely seen probing the marsh in some secluded cove; many a day in Sapling Prairie is enriched by the loud, musical, clattering rattle of their cries.

Pond Cypresses surround Big Water Lake.

Sapling Prairie gradually becomes more wooded as the rumpled forest increases its presence. Beyond mile 16 the prairie is reduced to isolated pockets and dwindling patches. Sedges, yellow-eyed grasses, Fragrant Water Lily, and Neverwet grow in the sunny openings and tree-speckled meadows that dot the shady woods.

Near mile 17, a grand cypress grove rises up and towers over the trail. The tall, old monarchs are adorned with draping banners of Spanish Moss. With little evidence of man's influence and few signs to mark the ages, it is easy to lose track of the centuries in these woods—the way it is easy to lose track of the days in other parts of the swamp.

At mile 17.7 you reach Dinner Pond. The narrow, 0.2-mile-long lake is so named because it was a convenient spot for the old Swampers to stop and have lunch. (The Swampers were early settlers of the swamp, living in and around the Okefenokee from the 1850s to the 1940s.) Then, as now, the little lake makes a pleasant place to take a break. There is even a small platform along the eastern side, which offers the opportunity to get out of your boat. Just before the end of the lake, the trail jogs to the left (east) and curves through a Titi thicket.

After Dinner Pond you pass through the last, shrubby remnants of Sapling Prairie. Then the trail jogs to the southeast and enters an extensive swamp forest. A thin overstory of Pond Cypress grows over the thick tangle of Swamp Bay, Dahoon Holly, and Hurrah Bush. It is a great tour of the transition from prairie to woodland as the shady forest closes in upon the trail.

Progressing into the forest, the trail narrows to a curvy, 4- to 8-foot-wide, creeklike channel. Thick shrubs, clumps of Swamp Loosestrife, and patches of sedges and grasses border the trail. Depending on water levels, you might notice a slight current flowing south toward Billys Lake.

For the next 0.7 mile the trail twists and turns through the dense forest. Use extra care as you navigate the tight passes and avoid overhanging branches and submerged stumps and logs. If you keep alert and maintain a controlled pace, you should have little difficulty. At low water, however, the narrow passage could cause some trouble.

Near mile 19 the forest canopy spreads back from the trail. The thick, shady woods retreat to the periphery, allowing Maidencane, Walter's Sedge, and yellow-eyed grasses to grow along the sunny edges of the widening channel. The Middle Fork of the Suwannee River literally forms beneath your boat as innumerable tributaries join the main watercourse. Almost magically the narrow, twisty channel transforms first to broad creek and then to winding river.

By mile 20 the river is 20 to 40 feet wide and laced with irregular bands of Spatterdock. Grasses, sedges, and ferns grow along the fringes and are backed by a cypress forest. Typical of the Okefenokee, the surrounding woods are either hushed in stillness or alive with the squawks, melodies, and catcalls of numerous birds: warblers, woodpeckers, thrushes, sparrows, hawks, and herons.

The Big Water overnight shelter.

Then just as it formed, the Middle Fork of the Suwannee mysteriously ravels into a braidwork of tiny branches as the river passes over a low rise. The trail follows the main channel, which narrows to 6 to 12 feet wide but before long, the river begins to broaden again, and the braided waterways gather back into the main course. This is the Okefenokee's less energetic version of the riffle-and-pool hydrography common on faster flowing streams.

At mile 21 you reach Big Water Lake, or simply Big Water. Here the river widens to a 75- to 100-foot-wide, open-water lake. Mature Pond Cypresses rise up from the shores and reflect on the surface of the tannin-stained water. This is the characteristic swamp that many people picture when envisioning the Okefenokee—majestic, primeval, and seductive. Do not become too entranced, because there are usually an abundance of submerged and partially submerged logs in the lake. Since the water is dark, they are difficult to see. The best course of action is a leisurely and cautious paddle through the area. Besides, a slow pace will give you the opportunity to savor the scenery and watch for the numerous alligators that inhabit the lake.

The Red Trail is open to day-use boating from the top of Big Water Lake to Stephen C. Foster State Park, so you may encounter other swamp visitors along this part of the trail. However, the few that may have ventured this far from the park are likely to have headed back to the boat ramp by the time you arrive.

In about 0.5 mile the lake constricts and passes through a shady grove of Pond Cypress, Swamp Bay, and Dahoon Holly. Then the river opens back up to the sluggish, open water of Big Water Lake. The broad "lake" meanders through the surrounding cypress forest with tranquil beauty. Green bands of Spatterdock stripe the shallow edges, and in fall and winter Dahoon Holly adds a splash of color with its cheery, red berries.

The holly berries are a favorite food of overwintering flocks of American Robins. Some winter days are alive with the full vigor of spring as they descend by the hundreds on the fruit-laden trees and fill the air with their chittering, chiming, and singing. At any time of year you can expect to find Wood Ducks, Belted Kingfishers, Pileated and Red-bellied Woodpeckers, Northern Cardinals, and Common Grackles.

Near mile 23, a small day-use platform lies on the eastern side of the river. The covered platform sits in the shady woods and is surrounded by cypress, hollies, and Hurrah Bush. The Big Water overnight shelter is about 1 mile farther down the trail.

In another 0.5 mile the lake constricts slightly, to about 40 to 60 feet wide. Along the wooded shores you find Red Maple, Swamp Bay, Dahoon Holly, Hurrah Bush, Titi, and of course Pond Cypress. You will probably notice a slight current in the river (0.5 to 2 miles per hour). Gliding along with the gentle current, it is hard to think of a more relaxing way to end the day than a quiet paddle on the lazy upper reaches of the Suwannee.

At mile 24.1 you reach the junction with the Red Trail Spur, which takes you to the Big Water overnight shelter. Watch for the signs and take the trail that enters the river on the eastern (left) side. From here, it is only 0.1 mile to the platform.

The Big Water overnight platform sits adjacent to the trail. It is in good condition and has a convenient step along the front. A young woodland of cypress, hollies, and bays wraps around the back and sides, giving it a secluded feel and offering protection from storms. Across the trail to the front, there is a nice stand of young cypress. Unfortunately a sign and water level gauge detract from the scenery directly opposite the platform.

According to the shelter's log, a number of canoeists have had encounters with the local alligators, which also use the platform. You can't blame them; it's a nice hauling out place for all. Just use a little extra caution and good 'gator manners (see "Alligators," page 15).

3 Big Water Shelter to Green Trail Junction along Red Trail Spur (toward Floyds Island)

Distance: 2 miles.

See map on page 124

Difficulty: Moderate.
Type of trail: Boat trail.
Hazards: Peat quagmires, lightning, heat exhaustion, airboats, biting insects.
Habitats: Prairie, shrubland, wooded swamp.
Reliability: Moderate to good.
USGS maps: Billys Island-GA, Dinner Pond-GA.
Visitor use: Light; permit required.

Overview: This 2-mile section of trail travels southward across Floyds Prairie to its junction with the Green Trail in the heart of the prairie. At the Big Water shelter (mile 0.1), the trail passes from swamp forest into a mosaic of prairie, shrubs, and woodlands. Wood Ducks dabble along the wooded edges; Sandhill Cranes and White Ibis wade the grassy prairies; and Red-shouldered Hawks hunt from the shrubby islands. Sometimes, alligators can be seen sunning along the trail in spring and fall. Since travel is limited to permit holders and refuge staff, you will have a good chance of paddling this part of the Okefenokee wilderness in solitude. The trail is occasionally closed due to drought.

The trail: From the Big Water overnight shelter continue southeast down the Red Trail Spur away from the Suwannee River. The quiet, winding boat trail cuts a path 5 to 10 feet wide through a shady forest of Pond Cypress, hollies, and Titi. A few Loblolly Bay and a few small pockets of sedges and grasses are scattered about in the mix. Barred Owls, Pileated Woodpeckers, Blue Jays, Gray Catbirds, Carolina Wrens, and Yellow-throated Warblers (summer) make their homes in the swampy woodland.

The surrounding woods gradually thin as you make the leisurely approach to Floyds Prairie. By mile 0.6 the cypress has begun to break up into stands with patches of sedges and Titi filling the gaps. Soon swaths of Walter's Sedge and patches of Fragrant Water Lily, Spatterdock, and Neverwet grow along the trail.

Floyds Prairie never opens into broad expanses of sedge glades and water lily pools. Instead, it maintains a patchy blend of woods and prairie throughout. Pond Cypress and Hurrah Bush form broken stands bordered with Titi and bamboo vine. The unforested areas between are filled with a blend of sedges, Maidencane, yellow-eyed grasses, Fragrant Water Lily, and Neverwet.

Numerous small pools attract a variety of wading birds (herons, egrets, and ibis), and you may spot a flock of endangered Wood Stork. Marsh Rabbit and even White-tailed Deer can be found in the juxtaposition of forest and prairie. Alligators and aquatic turtles can sometimes be seen warming themselves in sunny locations on the trail banks in spring and fall.

At mile 2.1 you reach the junction of the Green Trail with the end of the Red Trail Spur. Though just a short jaunt, you have already paddled most of the way across Floyds Prairie. Those on their way to Floyds Island will turn east (left) onto the Green Trail and follow it 1.8 miles to the island (see Trip 9, page 63).

4 **Big Water Shelter to Green Trail Junction along Red Trail (toward Stephen C. Foster State Park)**

Distance: 2.1 miles.

See map on page 125

Difficulty: Easy to moderate.
Type of trail: Boat trail, natural channel.
Hazards: Motorboats, airboats, alligators, biting insects.
Habitats: Wooded swamp.
Reliability: Moderate.
USGS map: Dinner Pond-GA.
Visitor use: Light to moderate; day-use boating permitted.

Overview: From the Big Water shelter this 2.1 mile section of trail follows a gently flowing stretch of the Suwannee River south to the junction with the Green Trail at the southwestern entrance to Floyds Prairie. Though the trail is open to public motorboat use, few day visitors travel this far from Stephen C. Foster State Park. As with any trail in the Suwannee River drainage, moderate drought can cause the trail to be closed.

The trail: From the Big Water overnight shelter head west for 0.1 mile on the wooded Red Trail Spur to the Suwannee River. At the river the Red Trail Spur meets the main path of the Red Trail (mile 24.1). Turn left (southwest) and follow the river downstream along the Red Trail. Truly a river to savor, the Middle Fork of the Suwannee River is easy to paddle and very scenic. The wooded riverbanks

A Pond Cypress forest along the Middle Fork of the Suwannee River.

are lined with Pond Cypress, Dahoon Holly, Titi, and Hurrah Bush. In a few places, strips of sedges and Maidencane manage to take root in the slack water along the edges. The flow is typically slow, as the dark waters wend their way through the swamp forest.

From mile 24.5 to mile 26 the river is broad and sweeping. Alligators and aquatic turtles are common but spend most of their time staying inconspicuous with just their heads or noses poking out of the dark water. During spring and fall, however, you may see them sunning along the banks or on exposed logs. Watch for Pileated Woodpeckers, Blue Jays, Common Grackles, Great Crested Flycatchers (summer), and Eastern Phoebes (winter) in the surrounding forest. Yellow-throated Warblers, and Northern Parulas enliven the trip during spring and early summer with their bright songs and colorful plumages.

At mile 26.1 you reach the southwestern entrance to Floyds Prairie. The terminus of the Green Trail enters on the east side of the river.

5 Green Trail Junction to Stephen C. Foster State Park

Distance: 5.7 miles.
Difficulty: Moderate.
Type of trail: River, natural channel.
Hazards: Motorboats, airboats, lightning, alligators, biting insects.
Habitats: Wooded swamp, lake.
Reliability: Moderate.
USGS maps: Billys Island-GA, Dinner Pond-GA.
Visitor use: Moderate to heavy; day-use boating permitted.

See map on page 125

Overview: This section of the Red Trail follows the winding path of the Suwannee River as it flows southwest through wooded forests of bays, maple, and cypress to Stephen C. Foster State Park. Along the way you will cross two lakes and pass beneath some of the most beautiful stands of mature cypress in the swamp. This is a good stretch of trail to see alligators and that strange southern bird, the Anhinga. Also watch for White Ibis, Wood Ducks, and Wood Storks. It is a popular section of trail, so expect to encounter other visitors, particularly along the portion from Minnies Lake to Stephen C. Foster State Park. This trail is occasionally closed due to low water.

The trail: From the Red Trail's junction with the Green Trail at mile 26.1 continue down the Middle Fork of the Suwannee River along the Red Trail. In about 0.5 mile the river narrows as it makes its way through a stand of mature cypress and thick shrubs. Regular boat traffic combined with the sharply winding nature of the river has lead to an accumulation of scars on the bases of many of the trees. From here to Billys Lake, the number of scars on the trees is a good indication of the sharpness of the curve ahead. Try to paddle slowly enough so that you do not add to the already numerous injuries.

51

Minnies Lake, on the Middle Fork of the Suwannee.

The trail winds through the shrubby forest until mile 27.4, where the river opens to the attractive scenery of Minnies Lake. About 1 mile long, the narrow lake is surrounded by a picturesque cypress forest. Alligators, Great Egrets, Little Blue Herons, and Anhingas are regularly found on the lake. Peripheral to the main channel, much of the lake is covered with a dense growth of Spatterdock. Anglers like to cast their lines into these waters, and you will find a steady increase in motorboat traffic from Minnies Lake to the end of the trail.

A small day-use rest shelter is located at the base of the lake on the northwestern side of the trail. The covered, 12-foot by 14-foot platform offers a nice place to take a paddling break and relax in the shady woods.

Past Minnies Lake the river narrows to 20 to 40 feet wide as it continues its serpentine path through the swamp forest. Pond Cypress, Red Maple, Dahoon Holly, and Swamp Bay share the banks with Titi and Hurrah Bush. Spatterdock, Neverwet, Maidencane, and spikerushes grow in irregular patches along the trail.

Within 0.5 mile, the bays, maple, and Dahoon Holly become less prevalent, and the cypress forest becomes the dominant feature. The next 1.5 miles hold some of the nicest views of mature cypress in the swamp. You paddle beneath, around, and between these large graceful trees as the river twists, curves, and divides its way along. Sharp, narrow bends alternate with broad, gentle curves on this portion of trail.

During the warm months sulphur butterflies, Tiger Swallowtails, and Emerald Jewelwings flit across the dappled sunlight of the shaded river course. Alligators and aquatic turtles sun along the shores in spring and fall, retiring to the concealment of the dark water during the heat of summer. Yellow-throated and

Prothonotary Warblers are often seen during the breeding season, being replaced by Eastern Phoebes, American Robins, and Yellow-rumped Warblers in the winter. Watch for Wood Ducks, White Ibis, Blue Jays, and Common Grackles throughout the year.

At mile 30.3 you reach the well-known and well-used Billys Lake. The Red Trail enters the lake on the north shore along the eastern end. At the lake turn right and head west, following the common paths of both the Red and Orange trails across the lake toward Stephen C. Foster State Park.

You can expect to encounter any variety of people on Billys Lake: motorboat and tour boat operators, anglers, canoeists, and kayakers. There are many reasons for the lake's popularity, though none probably more influential than its natural charm. You will not soon forget an evening paddle on Billys Lake with the glassy surface of the dark waters reflecting a mix of sunset colors and the images of tall, moss-cloaked cypresses.

The lake is surrounded by a forest of Pond Cypress, Loblolly Bay, and Sweetbay Magnolia. Scattered along the shore are groups and stragglers of large, mature cypresses. Their presence gives the lake its timeless quality. Most of the lake surface is free of vegetation, though numerous little Spatterdock-covered coves add variety to the shoreline.

Many alligators make their home on Billys Lake, and it is also a good place to view other wildlife, such as Ospreys, Belted Kingfishers, Anhingas, Pied-billed Grebes (winter), Wood Ducks, White Ibis, Great Blue Herons, and a variety of aquatic turtles. In the spring, look for Prothonotary and Yellow-throated Warblers amid the Pond Cypress. It is a good idea to stay close to the shores because motorboat traffic and wind can raise significant waves on the surface of the lake. Staying close to shore will also increase your chances of seeing wildlife, especially along the coves.

At mile 31.4, watch for the signs directing you to the 0.4-mile-long canal on the south shore of the lake, which leads to the end of the Red Trail at the boat basin at Stephen C. Foster State Park.

GREEN TRAIL

6 Kingfisher Landing to Bluff Lake Shelter

Distance: 7.6 miles.

See map on page 126

Difficulty: Moderate.
Type of trail: Canal, boat trail.
Hazards: Peat quagmires, lightning, heat exhaustion, motorboats, airboats, biting insects.
Habitats: Prairie, shrubland, wooded swamp, lake.
Reliability: Good.
USGS maps: Double Lakes-GA, Chase Prairie-GA.
Visitor use: Light to moderate; day-use boating permitted.

Overview: This section of trail begins at Kingfisher Landing on the northeastern side of the Okefenokee. It wends its way south along the eastern edge of the swamp through Durdin Prairie to the overnight shelter that sits just west of Bluff Lake. Durdin Prairie, a wonderful tract of sedge glades, sprawling shrublands, and cypress domes, is one of the most botanically rich areas of the swamp. With less open water than is found in other prairies, Durdin is more marshlike. Its soupy, often floating, peat mats and moderately fluctuating water levels provide conditions that support characteristic bog plants like pitcher plants, Narrow-leaved Sundew, Hatpins, and mats of sphagnum mosses. It is probably the best place to see Grass Pinks, which bloom in April and May. Great Egrets, Sandhill Cranes, Common Yellowthroats, Swamp Sparrows, Florida Cricket Frogs, and Carpenter Frogs can be seen or heard in season. Alligators are present but less likely to be seen. Though open to public day-use, you are likely to cross paths with other boaters only on occasion. Stable water levels make this one of the most dependable sections of trail in the swamp.

The trail: The put-in is at the Kingfisher Landing boat ramp. There is a parking lot and plenty of room for setting out your gear and getting organized. However, this area is an access point only and does not have the facilities that either Stephen C. Foster State Park or Suwannee Canal Recreation Area provide. Make certain that you have everything you need (including water) before arriving. Usually there is a composting toilet at the landing, but if there isn't, use the portable toilet that you brought for relief en route. Don't be tempted to use the woods.

Day-use boating is permitted on the trail to a point just beyond the Bluff Lake shelter, so you may encounter other visitors at the landing, in the canals, and along the trail. In practice, few day-use boaters venture farther than the end of the canal at mile 2.4, though you could cross paths with other permit holders travelling in the opposite direction. Overall, this area receives less use than either Stephen C. Foster State Park or Suwannee Canal Recreation Area.

The trail begins in the old Kings Canal, the first mile of which is the common path of both the Green and Red trails. A remnant of bygone peat mining operations of the 1950s, the canal is 40 to 50 feet wide and easy to paddle. If you are paddling while the air is still and the water calm, you will be treated to wonderful reflections of pine, hollies, myrtle, and bays on its open waters.

Paddling down the trail you pass an assortment of trees and shrubs. A broken overstory of Slash Pine, Loblolly Bay, Sweetbay Magnolia, and Dahoon Holly grows over a dense undergrowth of Titi, Hurrah Bush, Wax Myrtle, and Swamp Fetterbush. The character of the surrounding woods tends to be schizophrenic. Northern Cardinals, Eastern Towhees, Tufted Titmice, and others either fill the woods with nervous clatter or leave it lifeless and hushed. The sharp cackle of a Pileated Woodpecker that goes hardly noticed amid the ruckus of a sunny morning is startling as it pierces the silence of a thick fog.

Durdin Prairie offers a subtle landscape worth exploring.

At mile 0.4, avoid the short spur canal that jogs off from the southern side of the trail. Instead, watch for and turn left (south) down the Green Trail (toward Bluff Lake) at mile 1. Here a few Slash Pines, Dahoon Hollies, and bays manage to grow among the thick shrubs, and patches of yellow-eyed grasses, Maidencane, water lily, and Spatterdock nestle along the edges. Swamp Sparrows (winter), Common Yellowthroats, and White-eyed Vireos often scold passersby from the safety of the shrubs. Alligators can sometimes be found in the deep water of the canal.

At mile 1.5, take the right (west) fork of the canal, which opens to a swath of shrubby prairie. Hatpins, Hooded Pitcher Plants, and water lilies grow along the edge of the trail. Amid the shrubs and pools to the west you may find Red-winged Blackbirds, Wood Ducks, or perhaps a lone Little Blue Heron.

In another 0.4 mile, take the short jog to the right (west again) and follow the last leg of the canal around to the south. If you keep an eye on the trail markers and stay to the west after making the initial turn at mile 1.0, you should stay on track (see map inset, page 126).

Very near the end of the canal at mile 2.4, turn right (west) onto the narrower boat trail that will take you the rest of the way to Bluff Lake. Here you enter the expanse of trees, shrubs, and forbs called Durdin Prairie. Shrub-islands of Titi, Hurrah Bush, and Swamp Fetterbush are interspersed among sweeping marshy glades of sedges, yellow-eyed grasses, and Broomsedge. Sprinkled across the scene, small pockets of open water hold Fragrant Water Lily, Neverwet, and bladderworts.

Beyond the canal the trail is 6 to 10 feet wide and typically 2 to 3 feet deep. The trail has a tendency to fill with Watershield, bladderworts, and Fragrant Water Lily, particularly by the end of summer. Pushing your way through the encroaching vegetation can make paddling slow. How much glide you are able to get out of each stroke will depend almost entirely on how much vegetation is in the trail.

Paddling through Durdin Prairie you find that its special charm lies in subtle intricacy. It doesn't have the largest trees, the grandest lakes, or the most abundant wildlife. But everywhere you look, little threads reveal the fabric of life that flows through the swamp. A trampled patch of Walter's Sedge leads your eyes to the dome-shaped nest of a Round-tailed Muskrat and the discarded bits of last night's supper. The stump of a lightning-struck Pond Cypress gains new life with the growth of Swamp Fetterbush sprouting from its decaying wood. A flowering tuft of Trumpet Leaf Pitcher Plant catches your attention, but as you look closer you see the glistening leaves of a narrow-leaved Sundew on the elevated ground of its base. Looking closer still, you find a tiny fly struggling for its life to escape the sundew's sticky snares. Durdin Prairie is a living lesson in ecology, a little reminder of just how each square foot of earth comes to be unique.

Past mile 3 the shrub-islands become more sprawling and the clumps of cypress and pine more prominent. Durdin Prairie's botanical richness is evidenced by Hooded Pitcher Plant, Swamp Loosestrife, Neverwet, Hatpins, Arrow Arum, and Grass Pink. Watch for Great Egrets, Wood Ducks, and a myriad of Florida Cricket Frogs along the trail and in the adjacent prairie. After bearing left (east), the trail makes a short pass through a corridor of shrubs, then opens to reveal patches of Walter's Sedge, Chain Fern, Broomsedge, and yellow-eyed grasses interspersed among the low shrubs.

Between mile 4 and mile 6, the trail traverses a mixture of shrubs and emergent prairie. Carpets of sphagnum mosses and numerous clumps of pitcher plants grow on large, soggy mats of peat. All three species of the Okefenokee's pitcher plants can be seen from the trail: Trumpet Leaf with its tall, pale green, parasol-topped tubes; Hooded with its monkish, erect, covered stalks; and Parrot with its reclining, bulb-headed stems. Much of the peat in this part of the prairie is either floating or semifloating, so be extremely careful if you must exit your boat.

At mile 4.3 you cross the minuscule Flag Lake. Then the trail passes through a thin stand of Loblolly Bay and along a short corridor of Swamp Fetterbush and Hurrah Bush. Beyond, the trail returns to the shrubby mixture of Titi, Swamp Fetterbush, Broomsedge, yellow-eyed grasses, and Walter's Sedge. Watch for Gray Catbirds, Northern Mockingbirds, Carolina Wrens, and Common Yellowthroats in the protective cover of the shrubs.

Near mile 5.5 you pass a few small clumps of cypress and skirt the edge of a mature, moss-grown stand. After the cypress, the vista opens up. Sedge glades dotted with shrub and cypress islands are interspersed with flooded pools of water lily and Neverwet. The open marshes attract Great Egret, Little Blue Heron, Great Blue Herons, White Ibis, and Red-shouldered Hawks.

A camper at the Bluff Lake shelter hangs food where animals won't reach it.

At mile 6.5 you reach Durdin Lake. Though moderately sized with open water in its center and a wide fringe of Spatterdock along one edge, Durdin Lake does not attract much wildlife. Frogs are plentiful in the adjacent prairie, but the lake itself is more likely to be quiescent. The trail skirts the northeastern edge; but if you feel venturesome, you can take a short excursion around the lake. After the lake, the trail continues through approximately equal amounts of yellow-eyed grasses, sedges, Titi, and Broomsedge.

At mile 7.4 you reach Bluff Lake, an 8-acre, open-water lake that is fringed with a thick border of shrubs and a smattering of Spatterdock. While not particularly rich in wildlife, the lake is home to alligators, Pig Frogs, and Green Treefrogs. The trail's path cuts directly west across the lake to the far shore. Beyond the lake, it is only another 0.1 mile to the overnight shelter (mile 7.6), which sits alongside the trail.

Note that there is an unmarked spur trail that leaves the southeastern shore of Bluff Lake adjacent to the Green Trail. While not likely to cause trouble on a trip to the shelter, it could be confusing if you were heading toward Kingfisher Landing. This little, unmarked trail follows a swath of sedges 0.3 mile down to the crescent-shaped Half Moon Lake, a sprawling, Spatterdock-covered lake that hosts more Pig Frogs, Florida Cricket Frogs, and alligators. The spur trail makes a great late-afternoon paddle if you have some time left over at the end of the day while camping at the Bluff Lake shelter.

The Bluff Lake shelter sits near a small cypress wood and is partially surrounded by a low Titi, Hurrah Bush, and bamboo vine (greenbrier) thicket. The area adjacent to the platform is fringed with pitcher plants, Broomsedge, yellow-eyed grasses, water lily, and sedges. The platform is serviceable but significantly warped. It is a favorite perch of the local vultures.

7 Bluff Lake Shelter to Blue Trail Junction

Distance: 7.6 miles.
Difficulty: Moderate to difficult.
Type of trail: Boat trail.

See map on page 127

Hazards: Peat quagmires, constricted passages, biting and stinging insects, lightning, heat exhaustion, airboats.
Habitats: Prairie, shrubland, wooded swamp.
Reliability: Moderate to good.
USGS maps: Billys Island-GA, Chase Prairie-GA, Double Lakes-GA.
Visitor use: Light; permit required beyond mile 7.8.

Overview: This lightly used 7.6-mile section of trail passes west out of Durdin Prairie into a thick swamp forest. It then crosses Territory Prairie and skirts the northern edge of Chase Prairie where it meets the Blue Trail. The diversity of wildlife reflects the varied habitats. Wading birds, Wood Ducks, and Florida Cricket Frogs can be found in the prairies; Pileated Woodpeckers, Barred Owls, Great Crested Flycatchers (summer), Blue Jays, and Prothonotary Warblers (summer) in the woodlands. Low water levels can make the section between Durdin and Territory prairies a slow and strenuous journey. The trail offers reliable solitude, since most of it is limited to permit holders and refuge staff.

The trail: From the Bluff Lake shelter, head southwest along the trail. Here at its fringes, Durdin Prairie is quite shrubby. Wood Ducks, Sandhill Cranes, and Great Egrets may be seen in the small openings of Fragrant Water Lily, yellow-eyed grasses, sedges, and Chain Fern that pepper the rambling growth of Titi and Hurrah Bush. As you paddle toward the western edge of the prairie, the surrounding cypress forest gradually closes in upon the trail.

In about 0.2 mile you reach the limit of day-use boating. Beyond this point you are likely to cross paths with other people only on occasion, namely other canoe parties with a permit, cooperating officials, or refuge staff.

At mile 8, leaving all traces of Durdin Prairie behind, you pass into a scrubby forest of cypress, Hurrah Bush, hollies, and bays. Here the trail narrows to a width of 5 to 6 feet and becomes winding and twisty. The next 1.7 miles present an almost continuous series of sharp bends and curves. The trail also becomes noticeably shallower (1 to 2 feet deep) and clogged with peat sediment. At low water levels paddling can be strenuous. Even with sufficient water, expect a slow pace as you navigate the tight curves. At many points there is not enough room to paddle effectively in the constricted channel, and you may find that poling is more practical. Poling is the way the old Swampers used to get around in the Okefenokee—just use your paddle to push off from the bottom and sides of the trail. It's not very graceful, but it gets the job done.

Around you the forest is constantly changing character. One moment you are in a scrubby forest; the next, in a thicket of Titi and Hurrah Bush. At other points you pass young stands of Pond Cypress and pines or small glades of yellow-eyed grasses and Maidencane. Woodland birds, such as Great Crested Flycatchers (summer), Prothonotary Warblers (summer), and a variety of woodpeckers, can be found during their respective seasons. A few alligators and Pig Frogs make their home in scattered pools along the trail.

From mile 8.7 to mile 9.7, you pass through a thicket of Hurrah Bush, Black Titi, Wax Myrtle, and hollies. Along the way, sunny open-canopied avenues alternate with shady shrub corridors. At times the shrubs completely envelop the trail, creating tunnel-like passages. Low-hanging branches and shrubs cause you to duck and scratch your way through some of the thickest parts. Eastern Towhees, Carolina Wrens, Hooded Warblers (summer), and White-eyed Vireos chatter and sing from the thick tangle of shady bushes.

At mile 9.7 you reach the eastern edge of Territory Prairie and for the next 3 miles pass through this small prairie irregularly divided by the surrounding swamp forest. Mixed-age stands of cypress and pine weave through scrambled openings of yellow-eyed grasses, Maidencane, sedges, Neverwet, and Fragrant Water Lily. Hooded Pitcher Plant, Chain Fern, Broomsedge, and Grass Pink are sprinkled across the scene.

The trail widens to 6 to 8 feet and becomes gently winding. Combined with a deeper channel (2 to 3 feet), less sediment, and a center lane relatively free of vegetation, paddling is considerably faster and easier.

Between mile 10 and mile 11, you pass a variegated mix of thin cypress woods, Slash Pine, and shrub-dotted prairie. Great Blue Herons, Little Blue Herons, and Great Egrets search for Pig Frogs, pygmy sunfishes, and Florida Cricket Frogs in the prairie openings. Red-bellied and Pileated Woodpeckers clamber up the tree trunks, hammering and poking for caterpillars and grubs. Great Crested Flycatchers (summer) perch on exposed limbs and dart at passing insects. Northern Parulas (summer), Common Yellowthroats, and Carolina Wrens scuttle among the trees and shrubs, gleaning little arthropods from the leaves and twigs. Also watch for the occasional Wood Stork, Sandhill Crane, White Ibis, or alligator.

The next 1.5 miles offer pleasant paddling and enjoyable scenery. Territory Prairie unfolds like a series of secret meadows. Broad patches and small pockets of sedges, grasses, Neverwet, and Fragrant Water Lily fill gaps in the surrounding cypress and pine forest.

As you approach its western boundary, the prairie becomes increasingly shrubby. By mile 12.8 you have left Territory Prairie altogether and have entered the dense head of shrubs and forest that separates Territory Prairie from Chase Prairie to the south and west. The trail narrows slightly as it twists its way through the dense vegetation. A thicket of Titi, hollies, bamboo vine, and Hurrah Bush lines the trail. Overhead, a thin overstory of Pond Cypress and pine occupies the canopy. Breaks in the thicket reveal scrubby openings and woodlands. Between the two prairies there is a noticeable current in the trail because of a significant water level gradient—one of the largest in the swamp.

In little less than 1 mile you reach the eastern edge of Chase Prairie where scattered pines dot a disarray of young Pond Cypress, sprawling shrubs, yellow-eyed grasses, sedges, and Chain Fern. From here to the junction with the Blue Trail you travel across the northern arm of the prairie. Though shrubbier than the main body of the prairie to the south, the northern arm still sports excellent prairie vistas. Broad swaths of Fragrant Water Lily, Neverwet, yellow-eyed grasses, Maidencane, and sedges can be found amid the backdrop of Titi and Hurrah Bush. Slash Pine and Loblolly Bay are scattered about or in clumps at the center of shrub-islands. You can expect to see typical prairie wildlife, such as Great Blue Herons, Great Egrets, Wood Ducks, White Ibis, and possibly Sandhill Cranes and Wood Storks. Florida Cricket Frogs and Pig Frogs are common. You may see, or more likely only hear, that tiniest of North American frogs, the Little Grass Frog. Not much bigger than a housefly, they can be very difficult to find. You will probably have better luck detecting them by their call—a repetitive, high-pitched, metallic creak.

At mile 15.2 you reach the junction with the Blue Trail. The trail junction is marked in both blue and purple to aid those heading toward Round Top (Purple Trail). Bear to the right (north) to continue along the Green Trail.

8 Blue Trail Junction to Floyds Island

Distance: 1 mile.
Difficulty: Moderate.
Type of trail: Boat trail.
Hazards: Heat exhaustion, biting and stinging insects, peat quagmires, airboats.
Habitat: Shrubland, wooded swamp.
Reliability: Good.
USGS map: Billys Island-GA.
Visitor use: Light; permit required.

See map on page 127

Overview: This short 1-mile section of the Green Trail veers northwest from the junction with the Blue Trail through a thick swamp forest to the overnight stop on Floyds Island. Watch for Wood Ducks, woodpeckers, and a variety of warblers. You are unlikely to encounter anyone else on the trail since use is limited to permit holders and refuge staff. A short, 0.3-mile portage is required to continue along the Green Trail beyond Floyds Island. Though not necessary, it is advantageous to have your gear well packed and easily transportable. The trail reliably holds sufficient water for paddling.

The trail: From the junction with the Blue Trail, bear to the north along the Green Trail. Chase Prairie soon recedes as you make your way into the thick belt of Pond Cypress, pine, and Loblolly Bay that borders Floyds Island. Occasional breaks in the forest canopy are occupied by shrubby thickets in an otherwise dense forest of

A paddler makes her way through the forest along the Green Trail near Floyds Island.

61

Loblolly Bay. A diverse selection of Sweetbay Magnolia, Loblolly Bay, Titi, Hurrah Bush, hollies, bamboo vine, and Poor-man's Soap forms the understory. The trail cuts a winding path 8 to 15 feet wide through the forest. For the most part, the trail is clear of vegetation, about 2 feet deep, and easy to paddle. There are spots where low shrubs and trees encroach upon and overhang the trail, and other spots where fallen leaves accumulate in thick mats and make paddling a challenge.

During summer, Tiger Swallowtail and Black Swallowtail butterflies flit across sunny spots in the trail. In summer also watch for Prothonotary Warblers and Northern Parulas. Pileated Woodpeckers, Carolina Wrens, and Barred Owls can be found throughout the year. During just about any stretch of suitable weather you might see alligators, turtles, Florida Cricket Frogs, and Bronze Frogs.

At mile 16.2 you reach the southeastern side of Floyds Island and dry land. Floyds Island is a large sand ridge that formed more than 2 million years ago when the Okefenokee was covered by the sea. Higher than the surrounding swamp, it supports a growth of Slash Pine and Saw Palmetto. There are also grand Live Oaks festooned with Resurrection Fern, tall Southern Magnolias, Water Oaks, and tangles of bamboo vine and Wax Myrtle. Spending the night on Floyds Island gives you the chance to explore this very different Okefenokee ecosystem.

Spending the night on Floyds has a couple of other advantages. One is the opportunity to sleep in the quaint, little, tin-roofed cabin, complete with fireplace and front porch. Another is the chance to walk around on something larger than a 20-foot by 28-foot platform.

The cabin sits on the portage trail about 250 yards from the southeastern side of the island. Before you start carrying your gear, you might want to walk the trail and see what kind of carts are available. Usually, there is some type of cart in the vicinity of the cabin that can make the task of hauling your gear a little easier. The cabin has four rooms and plenty of space for reorganizing gear, hanging clothes to dry, or gaining a little privacy from that trip companion who snores all night. A boy scout troop has adopted the cabin and helps maintain it. Other than being a bit musty, you should find it in good shape. The cabin does have a bit of a cockroach problem. Close up all of your food at night and don't leave any scraps behind to perpetuate the problem. If you are squeamish about cockroaches (they are really big in the South), you can always pitch a tent outside. Wilderness enthusiasts may take this option regardless, preferring the open air and stars.

In addition to the cabin, there is a fire pit with benches, a cooking grate, and a small picnic table. A composting toilet is located southeast of the cabin along the portage trail. The hand pump at the back of the cabin provides nonpotable water only and is known to contain high coliform (bacteria) concentrations. Though we don't recommend using water from the hand pump for drinking purposes, it is probably the one water source in the swamp where you can use a water purification filter effectively (make sure it removes bacteria). Refrain from the temptation to wash your dishes, or yourself, at the pump. The area is not properly equipped for washing, and attempts leave an unsightly and unsanitary mess. If you use water from the pump for washing, please do the actual washing away from the vicinity of the cabin and trail. As in any wilderness area, use biodegradable soap (or none at all) and scatter the wash water in the woods. Also, if you use the water from the pump for washing dishes, remember to rinse the dishes with safe "drinking" water to avoid the possibility of contamination. You may want to avoid this water source altogether.

The birdlife here is like that found in other wooded areas of the swamp. Look and listen for Red-bellied Woodpeckers, Barred Owls, Great Crested Flycatchers (summer), Carolina Wrens, Blue-gray Gnatcatchers, Northern Parulas (summer), and White-eyed Vireos. Mammals, being more secretive than their avian counterparts, are more easily detected by tracks and other sign. White-tailed Deer leave dainty hoof prints with pointed tips. On the sandy substrate of the island they often register as indistinct pockmarks. Raccoons leave delicate hand-shaped tracks with their front feet and elongated tracks with their hind ones. The round, clawless tracks of a Bobcat are like those of a house cat, only larger. You may get to see a Raccoon, a deer, or even a Bobcat while on Floyds Island. In your wanderings be alert for rattlesnakes. Also, with Raccoons about, it is important not to leave any food unattended or improperly stored.

Floyds Island is a popular destination, and after staying there you will know why. In fact, you will probably find yourself wishing you could stay more than just one night.

The Green Trail continues on the northwestern side of the island. From the cabin it is only about 100 yards to the canoe trail. There are numerous camp trails emanating from the cabin, so scout the trail to make sure that you are on the correct one before hiking your canoe all over the island.

9 Floyds Island to Red Trail Spur Junction

Distance: 1.8 miles.

See map on page 124

Difficulty: Moderate.
Type of trail: Boat trail.
Hazards: Peat quagmires, heat exhaustion, biting and stinging insects, lightning, airboats.
Habitat: Prairie, shrubland, wooded swamp.
Reliability: Moderate.
USGS map: Billys Island-GA.
Visitor use: Light; permit required.

Overview: This 1.8-mile section of the Green Trail travels northwest from the dry shore of Floyds Island to the junction with the Red Trail Spur in the middle of Floyds Prairie. It takes you from a high sandy island, through a thick swamp forest, and across a mixture of woodlands and shrubby prairie. Watch for White-tailed Deer, Great Egrets, Sandhill Cranes, Red-shouldered Hawks, Red-bellied Woodpeckers, and Yellow-throated Warblers (summer). Public access is limited to permit holders,

Portaging across Floyds Island.

keeping visitor use to a minimum. Even though the trail holds water after the surrounding prairie has begun to dry, this trail is occasionally closed due to drought.

The trail: From mile 16.5 on the northwestern side of the Floyds Island the trail begins in a mature woodland of Pond Cypress and Loblolly Bay. For the next 0.5 mile, the 5- to 8-foot-wide trail is overhung with thick vegetation. A tall forest canopy looms overhead; dense shrubs line parts of the trail and lean in heavily from the sides. The woods, though at times quiet and gloomy, are home to a variety of birds. Barred Owls, Red-bellied Woodpeckers, Carolina Wrens, Blue Jays, and Gray Catbirds can be found year-round. Great Crested Flycatchers, Red-eyed Vireos, Northern Parulas, and Yellow-throated Warblers add their songs in spring and summer.

Before long you notice that the forest is thinning and losing stature. Stepping away from Floyds Island, the Loblolly Bay forest gradually changes to a low, scrubby woodland. Dahoon Holly, Hurrah Bush, and Swamp Fetterbush grow in the understory and occupy gaps in the canopy.

A little past mile 17 you reach the eastern edge of Floyds Prairie. Thickets and tangles alternate with shrubby tunnels and wooded canopies. Gaps in the corridor provide occasional views into thin woodlands, marshy meadows, and shrubby clearings. The wooded marshes along the trail often attract overwintering flocks of Sandhill Cranes. The dense vegetation makes it difficult to catch sight of them, but you can still enjoy the sound of their quiet murmurings and raucous calls.

In another 0.5 mile the shrubs and trees abate somewhat. Sedges and Maidencane share the growing prairie with Neverwet and Fragrant Water Lily. Floyds Prairie, with its mosaic of cypress woods, grassy strips, and water lily pools, offers continually changing scenery and varied wildlife. A break in the trees may reveal a flock of White Ibis probing their sickle-shaped bills among the grasses. A Red-shouldered Hawk may pass overhead, filling the air with its screeching cries. Or perhaps you may come upon a whitetailed doe and her fawn belly-deep in the prairie feeding on the succulent, watery growth.

At mile 18.3 you reach the junction with the Red Trail Spur. To the north, the Red Trail Spur leads 2.0 miles to the Big Water overnight shelter. The Green Trail continues to the west through Floyds Prairie.

10 Red Trail Spur Junction to Red Trail Junction

Distance: 1.3 miles.

See map on page 124

Difficulty: Moderate.
Type of trail: Boat trail.
Hazards: Peat quagmires, lightning, heat exhaustion, airboats, biting insects.
Habitat: Prairie, shrubland, wooded swamp.
Reliability: Moderate.
USGS maps: Billys Island-GA, Dinner Pond-GA.
Visitor use: Light; permit required.

Overview: This 1.3-mile section of the Green Trail meanders west across Floyds Prairie until reaching the Suwannee River at the Red Trail junction. On the way, the trail passes a checkerboard of woods and prairie as it follows a scenic course along the southern extent of Floyds Prairie. A variety of wildlife can be seen: alligators, Florida Cricket Frogs, White Ibis, Great Egrets, Sandhill Cranes, Red-shouldered Hawks, Carolina Wrens, and Common Yellowthroats. Public access is limited to permit holders, allowing the possibility of enjoying this prairie wilderness in solitude. The trail is sometimes closed due to drought.

The trail: From the junction with the Red Trail Spur at mile 18.3, veer southwest and continue along the Green Trail. As you enter the heart of Floyds Prairie, take a moment to look around. Like every prairie, Floyds has its own character. Nowhere are there large sedge meadows or expansive water lily pools. Nowhere are there dense, impenetrable woodlands or rolling thickets. Instead, wood and prairie intermingle in fluid balance. Titi-bordered stands of cypress and bays wind through the many sedge and water lily pools like a maze of woodland doorways opening to a myriad of hidden prairie rooms.

Wildlife is reflective of the mix of woods and prairie. Around one bend a deer may leap across the marsh; around another a startled Chain Pickerel might leap out of the water and into your boat. Barred Owls and Sandhill Cranes are equally at home, as are Marsh Rabbits and Pig Frogs.

From mile 18.3 to mile 19, you paddle across the southern portions of Floyds Prairie. A mature cypress forest is visible on the periphery as you follow the winding, 6- to 10-foot-wide boat trail through a mosaic of prairie, wood, and shrub.

Patches of emergent and water lily prairie intermingle with cypress woodlands in Floyds Prairie.

Neverwet, bladderworts, and Fragrant Water Lily occupy shallow open waters, whereas yellow-eyed grasses, sedges, and Maidencane crowd marshy glades. Ever present and opportunistic, Titi shrubs form low islands and fringe scattered groups of cypress.

Watch for Wood Ducks, White Ibis, and Little Blue Herons in the watery swales; Red-shouldered Hawks, Pileated Woodpeckers, and Carolina Wrens among the cypress; and Sandhill Cranes, Great Egrets, and Great Blue Herons in the grassy marshes. Wood Storks visit on their erratic schedule, found in flocks one week and completely absent the next. Alligators and aquatic turtles frequent the area but are not easily seen.

Past mile 19 the trail becomes more wooded. The once-separate cypress woodlands aggregate into a fenestrated forest, where tall, mossy trees and young clusters wrap around clumps of shrubs and pockets of water lily, sedges, and grasses. Some sections of the trail are quite shrubby, being lined with a thick growth of Dahoon Holly, Titi, Hurrah Bush, and Swamp Fetterbush. The broken forest attracts Wood Ducks, Northern Mockingbirds, Gray Catbirds, Northern Cardinals, Yellow-throated Warblers (summer), and a variety of woodpeckers.

At mile 19.6 you leave Floyds Prairie and reach the Middle Fork of the Suwannee River. Here the Green Trail ends. To reach Stephen C. Foster State Park, turn left (southwest) onto the Suwannee River and follow the Red Trail (see Trip 5, page 51).

BLUE TRAIL

11 Green Trail Junction to Purple Trail Junction

Distance: 0.8 mile.
Difficulty: Moderate.
Type of trail: Boat.
Hazards: Peat quagmires, lightning, heat exhaustion, strong winds, motorboats, airboats, biting insects.
Habitats: Prairie, shrubland.
Reliability: Good.
USGS maps: Chase Prairie-GA, Billys Island-GA.
Visitor use: Light; day-use boating permitted beyond mile 0.2.

See map on page 128

Overview: The Blue Trail links the Green, Purple, and Orange trails. This short section of it crosses a mix of prairie and shrubs as it passes southeast from its start at the Green Trail to the junction with the Purple Trail at mile 0.8. Watch for Wood Ducks, Red-shouldered Hawks, Ospreys, Turkey and Black Vultures, and a variety of wading birds (cranes, herons, egrets, ibis). All but the first 0.2 mile of the trail are open to public day-use boating, though you are unlikely to see other visitors. Water levels should be adequate for passage unless the Okefenokee is experiencing a substantial drought.

The trail: The trail begins at mile 15.2 of the Green Trail in the northwestern corner of Chase Prairie. It is best to avoid the unmarked cutoff to the west that crosses from mile 15.4 of the Green Trail to mile 0.2 of the Blue Trail. Instead, start the Blue Trail at its marked junction with the Green Trail at mile 15.2. You will notice that the Blue Trail is marked in both blue and purple at this junction. This is to help guide those on their way to Round Top.

The trail is 6 to 10 feet wide, about 2 feet deep, and mostly free of vegetation. It starts with a vista of Neverwet and Fragrant Water Lily, which tinge the prairie yellow in February (Neverwet) and white in summer (water lily) with their flowers. Sedges, yellow-eyed grasses, and Chain Fern fringe the many shrub-islands that dot the prairie. Slash Pine and Loblolly Bay are scattered throughout.

Take advantage of the open views and watch for the White Ibis, Great Egrets, and Great Blue Herons that frequent the prairie. Sandhill Cranes and, if water levels are favorable, Wood Storks can also be found. Carolina Wrens, Common Yellowthroats, Swamp Sparrows (winter), Gray Catbirds, and Eastern Phoebes (winter) can be seen and heard in the shrubby areas.

At mile 0.2 you will reach the "Permits Only/No Motors" sign, which signifies that the rest of the trail is open to public day-use motorboating and canoeing. Few day-use boaters use the trail, and you are likely to travel it in solitude.

Continuing, you pass areas crowded with Titi and Hurrah Bush alternating with those supporting a balance of prairie and shrub. Hooded Pitcher Plants form dense clusters in sunny locations along the trail, and if quiet you may surprise a pair of Wood Ducks or a flock of ibis at close range around one of the concealed bends.

By the time you reach the junction with the Purple Trail at mile 0.8, the vista has opened up again with prairie as the dominant feature. The vantage provides excellent views of the medley of shrub-islands and cypress stands that dot the plain.

12 Purple Trail Junction to Orange Trail Junction (Canal Run Shelter)

Distance: 1.8 miles.

See map on page 128

Difficulty: Moderate.
Type of trail: Boat trail, canal.
Hazards: Peat quagmires, lightning, heat exhaustion, strong winds, motorboats, airboats, biting insects.
Habitats: Prairie, shrubland, wooded swamp.
Reliability: Good.
USGS maps: Chase Prairie-GA, Billys Island-GA.
Visitor use: Light; day-use boating permitted.

Overview: This section of the Blue Trail takes a southward course across the western side of Chase Prairie. Starting in an open mix of prairie and shrub, the trail soon wends its way along the wooded, western edge of the prairie. The last bit follows a section of the Suwannee Canal to the junction with the Orange Trail. As is true of the rest of Chase Prairie, Sandhill Cranes, Great Egrets, White Ibis, and Red-shouldered Hawks frequent the area. Along the wooded prairie edge, you can find Wood Ducks, Red-bellied and Pileated Woodpeckers, Carolina Wrens, and a variety of warblers. Though the trail is open to day-use canoeing and motorboating, it receives only light use. Water levels are typically sufficient for paddling throughout the year.

The trail: From the junction with the Purple Trail at mile 0.8, the Blue Trail continues as a winding boat trail through the open mix of prairie and shrub that is characteristic of Chase Prairie. Still 6 to 10 feet wide, approximately 2 feet deep, and mostly free of vegetation, the trail offers pleasant paddling across the open landscape. Much of the prairie is covered by the floating pads of Fragrant Water Lily and the floppy "rabbit ears" of Neverwet. Yellow-eyed grasses, sedges, and pitcher plants crop up and form swaths that fringe the myriad of Titi and Hurrah Bush shrub-islands.

Watch for Sandhill Cranes, Great Egrets, Great Blue Herons, and White Ibis wading in the surrounding prairies. Florida Cricket Frogs favor these prairies as well, and can be found sitting out on lily pads or hiding amid the grasses and sedges. If you don't see one of these quarter-sized amphibians, listen for their calls, which sound remarkably like two marbles being tapped together.

Past mile 1 the trail hugs the wooded, western margin of Chase Prairie. A mature cypress forest lies to the west, and you get nice views of the trees as you weave in and out of the forest along the prairie border. The prairie, never far to the east, appears and disappears through gaps in the intervening cypress trunks. At intervals the trail emerges into the open air of the adjacent prairie, then returns to the sun-dappled shade of the cypress. The forest-prairie ecotone—the area of transition from prairie to forest—attracts a variety of birds. Watch for Wood Ducks, Little Blue Herons, Red-shouldered Hawks, Barred Owls, Eastern Phoebes (winter), Great Crested Flycatchers (summer), and a variety of woodpeckers and warblers.

A little past mile 2 you reach the northern arm of the Suwannee Canal and leave Chase Prairie. Turn left and follow the canal south. The canal is wide and easy to paddle. It is lined with a thick forest of Pond Cypress, bays, Wax Myrtle, Hurrah Bush, and Titi. Alligators like the deeper water of the canal, and you may see one or two along the way. It is 0.4 mile down the canal to the end of the Blue Trail at its junction with the Orange Trail. The Canal Run shelter is located on the Orange Trail about 0.2 mile to the west of the junction.

PURPLE TRAIL

13 Orange Trail Junction to Round Top Shelter

Distance: 2.5 miles.

See map on page 128

Difficulty: Moderate.

Type of trail: Boat trail.

Hazards: Peat quagmires, lightning, heat exhaustion, strong winds, airboats, biting insects.

Habitats: Prairie, shrubland, wooded swamp.

Reliability: Good.

USGS map: Chase Prairie-GA.

Visitor use: Light; permit required.

Overview: This section of the Purple Trail begins at the junction with the Orange Trail on the southwestern side of Chase Prairie. From the trail junction, it traverses east across Chase Prairie through a mixture of prairie and shrubs before arcing back to the north along a cypress forest to the overnight shelter at Round Top. In season, Chase Prairie hosts Blue-winged Teal (winter), Wood Ducks, Sandhill Cranes, Common Yellowthroats, alligators, and plenty of chorusing Florida Cricket Frogs. Chase Prairie is one of the oldest prairies in the Okefenokee, and this trail provides an excellent tour through it. Since water levels are reliable, the trail should be passable unless there has been unusually dry weather. Public access is limited to permit holders, so the Purple Trail is a good place to look for some solitude.

The trail: From mile 8.9 of the Orange Trail, turn east onto the Purple Trail and leave the Suwannee Canal. Chase Prairie welcomes you with an abrupt transition from the shady, tree-lined canal to the wide vistas of the open prairie. Narrower and more serpentine than the canal, the Purple Trail is 5 to 10 feet wide and about 2 feet deep. Although a variety of plants crowd the edges of the channel, the center of the trail stays relatively free of vegetation. Remember that out in the middle of the prairie you will have little protection from the elements. Strong winds can make paddling difficult and strenuous; sun and rain beat down without relief.

The first 1.5 miles across the prairie contain a scenic mix of prairie and shrubs. The round, floating leaves of Fragrant Water Lily and upright stalks of Neverwet, sedges, and yellow-eyed grasses form broad swaths around the compact growth of Titi and Hurrah Bush. Clusters of Loblolly Bay grow amid the larger shrub-islands, and to the south a large bay woodland lines the horizon.

Chase Prairie offers excellent wildlife watching. Sandhill Cranes, Great Blue Herons, Great Egrets, White Ibis, Blue-winged Teal (winter), and Wood Ducks frequent the open prairie. Turkey Vultures, Red-shouldered Hawks, and Ospreys soar overhead. Carolina Wrens, Common Yellowthroats, and Gray Catbirds flit among the shrubs. Frogs, especially the ubiquitous Florida Cricket Frog, abound. Alligators, though fairly common, are not usually seen.

Paddling on the Purple Trail through Chase Prairie.

In a way analogous to how geologists look at the earth's strata or botanists look at the annual rings of a tree, palynologists (pollen scientists) and petrographers (rock scientists) can look at the successive layers of the Okefenokee's peat and gain insight into when the swamp first formed and how it has changed over time. With the aid of a special device, small vertical cores are removed from the peat bed. Examination of these cores has revealed that Chase Prairie has not changed much since the Okefenokee Swamp first formed some five or six thousand years ago. As you paddle, take the time to savor this jewel of timeless nature. In the spring, especially, when the alligators are bellowing in earnest and their throaty rumbles resound across the prairie, you feel as though you are truly surrounded by nature primeval.

Approaching mile 2, a substantial forest of Pond Cypress rises ahead. Here the trail bends to the north and skirts the edge of the woods, which loom to the east in all forms. Flowing plumes of Spanish Moss drape gracefully from the tall, stately trees. To the west, prairie views still dominate in a roughly even mix of prairie and shrub. Tufts of Redroot and Hatpins mingle with Hooded Pitcher Plant, Grass Pink, Fragrant Water Lily, and yellow-eyed grasses. The smooth grasslike leaves of Redroot are similar to those of the more common yellow-eyed grasses, though wider. When in bloom (summer), its tightly-packed clusters of white flowers are easily distinguished from the long-stalked, yellow flowers of the yellow-eyed grasses. Redroot is a favorite food of Sandhill Cranes, and you may spy a pair quietly foraging on them in some secluded spot.

Between mile 2 and the Round Top shelter (mile 2.5) you cross a patchwork of prairie, shrubs, and forest. Skirting the edge of the cypress, you may see or hear Barred Owls, Northern Cardinals, Pileated Woodpeckers, Red-shouldered Hawks, and Great Crested Flycatchers (summer) in addition to the herons and egrets found in the prairie. Pond Cypress, hollies, Swamp Bay, and Loblolly Bay rise out of some of the larger shrub-islands. In May and June the rosy pink blossoms of Grass Pinks dot the prairie.

The Round Top overnight shelter sits in the middle of Chase Prairie and offers a great panorama. To the south and west, the prairie stretches before you. Clusters of Hurrah Bush and Titi grow amid the gamut of Neverwet, Fragrant Water Lily, sedges, and grasses. Small bunches of the tubelike leaves of Hooded Pitcher Plant are scattered across the scene. To the east, the characteristic flat-topped silhouette of mature Pond Cypress dominates the skyline. Nearer the platform some cypress grow on the many shrub-islands that dot the landscape.

Pig Frogs, Southern Leopard Frogs, and Florida Cricket Frogs flourish in the surrounding prairie. Throughout much of the year, you are likely to be treated to a front row seat for their chorus concerts. Taking the bass notes, Pig Frogs make deep grunting sounds that are often mistakenly attributed to alligators (alligators make a drawn-out roar). Southern Leopard Frogs fill in at tenor with a bizarre array of sounds that are, at best, difficult to describe. Their main mating call is a gurgling, staccato chuckle, but they also make rubbery, creaking sounds like those

The picnic table at Round Top shelter may be small but it has a great view.

of someone running their fingers across a large balloon. Florida Cricket Frogs add a percussive beat with their rhythmic clacking calls.

The Round Top shelter is spacious and in excellent condition. Combined with the beautiful setting, it is one of the nicest overnight stops in the swamp. However, because it sits out in the middle of the prairie it does not offer much protection from wind and blowing rain. Strong winds should be expected, so tie your tent down well and keep your gear and loose items secured. Extra rope is essential when trying to find suitable lash points on the wooden platform. Also, do not depend on the platform roof to keep you dry in a leaky tent. Wind can blow rain right under the roof, drenching the entire platform.

14 Round Top Shelter to Blue Trail Junction

Distance: 2.8 miles.

See map on page 128

Difficulty: Moderate.
Type of trail: Boat trail.
Hazards: Peat quagmires, lightning, heat exhaustion, strong winds, airboats, biting insects.
Habitats: Prairie, shrubland, wooded swamp.
Reliability: Good.
USGS map: Chase Prairie-GA.
Visitor use: Light; permit required.

Overview: From the Round Top shelter, this 2.8-mile section of trail follows a northwest course across Chase Prairie to the end of the Purple Trail at its junction with the Blue Trail. Along the way you pass through an expansive, open prairie peppered with a variable mix of Hurrah Bush and Titi shrub-islands. Chase Prairie attracts Wood Ducks, Red-shouldered Hawks, many wading birds, and a multitude of frogs. The trail usually holds enough water for paddling, and since it is limited to permit holders and refuge staff, it is a good place to find relief from the crowds.

The trail: From the shelter, the trail continues its winding path north and west across Chase Prairie. To the east the cypress forest remains prominent, providing a scenic backdrop for the expansive prairie that spreads westward from its feet. Irregular bands of sedges, yellow-eyed grasses, and Redroot intermingle with patches of Neverwet and Fragrant Water Lily to create sweeping prairie vistas. Like ships sailing the sea, the shrub- and tree-islands seem to float in the watery expanse. Red-shouldered Hawks, Pileated Woodpeckers, Wood Ducks, Great Egrets, and White Ibis can be found amid the combination of woods and prairie.

The winding boat trail is an ample 6 to 10 feet wide and typically more than 2 feet deep. Although overgrown at the edges, the center of the channel is mostly free of vegetation and easy to paddle. The main difficulty lies in the possibility of strong winds blowing across the open prairie. Though the prairie offers more protection than you would find in the middle of a large lake, strong winds can make paddling arduous.

Traveling from mile 4 to mile 5, you notice the character of the prairie change. The neat, compact growth of the shrub-islands becomes less contained as the trees and shrubs grow in larger patches and stands. At times Titi, Hurrah Bush, Loblolly Bay, and Pond Cypress relegate the prairie to fringes and strips. Still, the broad prairie vistas dominate. Great swaths and unfolding avenues of Fragrant Water Lily and sedges spread out on all sides. The tall bushy-topped stalks of Broomsedge sway in isolated clumps. The gently tapered leaves of Neverwet wave just above the water's surface.

In February, the unusual flowers of Neverwet cover the prairie like a thousand little candles. The slim, waxy spikes—technically called spadixes—with their burgundy bases, gleaming-white middles, and flaming-yellow tips glow incandescent in the low angle of the morning sun.

The extensive shallow prairies attract many species of wading birds. Keep a watchful eye for Great Blue Herons, Little Blue Herons, Great Egrets, Snowy Egrets, White Ibis, Sandhill Cranes, and the occasional Wood Stork.

Past mile 5, the character of the prairie alternates between the cluttered shrublands of Titi and Hurrah Bush and the open landscape of the prairies—each waxing and waning in diametrical proportion. The blend of shrubs and prairie makes for interesting paddling through the changeable scenery. Hooded Pitcher Plants become more prevalent along this stretch and can be found in scattered clumps around the bases of shrubs or along the fringes of the emergent grasses and sedges. Though particularly attractive when sporting their yellow blossoms in May and early June, pitcher plants are a marvel in any season. The tubelike

Neverwet in flower along the Purple Trail.

leaf contains a watery slurry that traps and dissolves small insects and arthropods. Minerals in the slurry are absorbed by the plant and provide supplementary sustenance in the nutrient-poor landscape of the swamp.

At mile 5.3 you reach the end of the Purple Trail at its junction with the Blue Trail. For those en route to the Green Trail, turn right and follow the Blue Trail northwest for about 0.8 mile to the Green Trail junction (see Trip 11, page 67). Along the way you will pass through a nice mix of prairie and shrubs.

ORANGE TRAIL

15 Suwannee Canal Recreation Area to Purple Trail Junction

Distance: 8.9 miles.
Difficulty: Easy.
Type of trail: Canal.
Hazards: Heat exhaustion, motorboats, airboats, alligators, biting insects.
Habitats: Wooded swamp.
Reliability: Good.
USGS maps: Chase Prairie-GA, Chesser Island-GA.
Visitor use: Moderate to heavy; day-use boating permitted.

See map on page 129

Overview: This 8.9-mile section of the Orange Trail begins at the Suwannee Canal Recreation Area on the eastern side of the swamp. From the boat ramp it follows the path of the Suwannee Canal west and north to its junction with the Purple Trail just southwest of Chase Prairie. For its entire length the trail lies within the confines of the tree- and shrub-lined canal. While not the most scenically varied of trails, the tannin-stained water provides marvelous reflections and easy paddling. Alligators, turtles, Great Blue Herons, Anhingas, and numerous warblers are just some of the wildlife to watch for. Since the canal is fairly deep (5 to 7 feet), only the most severe droughts cause water levels to drop sufficiently for the trail to become impassable. Beginning at one of the most heavily visited points in the refuge, the first several miles of the trail are well used and sometimes crowded. Beyond mile 2 the number of visitors declines steadily, and only on the busiest of days will you encounter many people more than a few miles from the boat ramp. The entire section of trail is open to day-use paddling and motorboating.

The trail: The put-in is at the boat ramp (a fee is charged) at the Suwannee Canal Recreation Area. There is a paved parking lot, picnic tables, pay telephone, restrooms, water fountains, visitor center, and concessionaire. The ramp and canal are open to tour boat, public motorboat, canoe, and kayak day-use, so expect to encounter other swamp visitors.

From the boat ramp, paddle out of the boat basin and bear right into the main channel of the canal. Keep to the right again and pass north around the small, wooded spit along the outgoing traffic route. This is probably the most heavily used area of the swamp, so be alert for other boaters as well as anglers on the shores. If you prefer to avoid the crowds, schedule your departure from Suwannee Canal Recreation Area for early in the morning, during a weekday, or both.

The Orange Trail follows the Suwannee Canal for 11 miles. The canal itself is the product of Captain Harry Jackson's ill-fated attempt to drain the swamp. Unfortunately for him, but fortunately for many of us, he was unsuccessful. The canal is 35 to 40 feet wide, mostly free of impeding vegetation, and easy to paddle. If you are an inexperienced paddler, or just a bit rusty, you will have some space to get the feel of your craft and work on your technique.

The spoil banks of the canal are lined with Pond Cypress, Slash Pine, Loblolly Bay, and Dahoon Holly. Cascading plumes of Spanish Moss drape from the tallest trees and wave heavily in the breeze. Underneath, a dense growth of Titi and Hurrah Bush fills the gaps, limiting your vista to the canal and occasional glimpses of adjacent prairies. The deep, tannin-stained, open water offers beautiful reflections of the tall trees.

Watch closely for alligators and Great Blue Herons. They often sit inconspicuously amid the small shrub openings at the edges of the canal. Anhingas, Black and Turkey Vultures, Northern Mockingbirds and a variety of wading birds can be seen flying overhead or perching in the trees along the trail. Sandhill Cranes regularly call from nearby prairies.

Following the canal you pass the junction with the Yellow Trail at mile 1.8. The Yellow Trail, which begins on the northern shore of the canal, is a day-use canoe trail that passes through Mizell Prairie.

At mile 1.9, the canal forks. Though both channels eventually rejoin, the Orange Trail follows the right fork and the more direct route to the northwest. The left fork continues west to Chesser Prairie before turning north and reconnecting with the right fork. The two canals form a rough triangle, hence the area is called the Triangle. The junction is well marked with a large sign and should not cause confusion. Take the right (northwest) fork toward Chase Prairie.

Approximately 0.2 mile past the fork there is a comfort station on the northeastern side of the trail, a welcome sight to those who didn't realize they needed one before they left the boat ramp. The vegetation on the banks starts off a bit scrubby then develops into a mix of mature Pond Cypress and pines. Watch for Blue-gray Gnatcatchers, Yellow-rumped Warblers (winter), Common Yellowthroats, Gray Catbirds, and American Goldfinches (winter) foraging in the shrubs and trees. The canal is noticeably narrower (15 to 20 feet) but still generously wide enough to avoid any feelings of claustrophobia.

At mile 3.1 the southern loop of the canal (southern side of the Triangle) reconnects with the trail. Your path continues straight (west) down the main path of the Suwannee Canal. Past the juncture, the trail widens to its former span of 35 to 40 feet. Here Loblolly Bay, with its thick, bluntly serrated leaves, and Sweetbay Magnolia, with its leathery silver-bottomed leaves, become more prevalent. Titi

Tall Pond Cypress and Slash Pine line the open waters of the Suwannee Canal.

and Hurrah Bush still occupy the understory with the help of an occasional Wax Myrtle.

Past mile 4 the stature of the trees increases. Pond Cypress replaces much of the Loblolly Bay, while the Titi and Hurrah Bush become overgrown with bamboo vine (greenbrier). Near mile 4.5 the trail narrows to 20 to 30 feet, and Loblolly Bay and Sweetbay Magnolia crowd out the Pond Cypress, only to have the cypress and Slash Pine rejoin them just before mile 5.

As you paddle this calm stretch of the trail you can get a good look at Okefenokee's unusual water. The first thing that strikes you is its dark color—blackwater. Trying to peer below the surface can be like looking into a dark cave on a moonless night. You know there are fishes and turtles and alligators down there, but you can't see them. Little topminnows (small fishes) break the surface and cause tiny ripples, but are virtually invisible scant millimeters below.

The dark color is somewhat of an illusion. If you scoop up a bit in a clear glass and hold it to the sun, you will find it more of a brownish amber. The soils of the swamp are unable to bind the fulvic acids (tannins) that leach from the fallen plant material. These tannins accumulate in the water, staining it like tea and increasing its acidity. The pH of the water can be as low as 3.1, though typically it ranges closer to 4.0.

Being in a swamp you might expect the water to be rancid, but it isn't. Old seafarers used to travel up the St. Marys just to fill their casks with Okefenokee's water because it remained fresh for long periods of time at sea, though it does have a somewhat bitter taste. (Nowadays you are better off carrying in your drinking water; see—"Drinking and Wash Water," page 8.)

The clear, open water of the Suwannee Canal is one of the best places to view the most famous aspect of Okefenokee's water—its reflectiveness. On calm, sunny days, images of sky, clouds, trees, and passing birds form on the mirrorlike surface with amazing clarity. Except for their subdued brightness, the reflections belie reality.

At mile 5.7 there is a day-use rest stop situated on the southwestern side of the canal. A covered table and composting toilet sit on the narrow spoil bank under a canopy of cypress and pine. It is a good place to stretch your legs or grab a bite to eat while listening to the seasonal choruses of Pig, Carpenter, and Florida Cricket Frogs in little Coffee Bay, which lies just to the west. The occasional Wood Duck can be found hiding among the secluded pools on the far side of the bank. The trees along the canal are a good place to spot Northern Parulas, Yellow-throated Warblers, and Prothonotary Warblers during the spring. You may be surprised to find a Gray Squirrel in the trees as well; not an animal generally associated with large swamps, Gray Squirrels do quite well in many areas of the Okefenokee. One other critter that you should keep a sharp look out for is the Raccoon. Though possessing many endearing traits, Raccoons can be quite a nuisance. We've had run-ins with determined Raccoons mooching at Coffee Bay, so keep your lunches out of their reach. Please, above all, never succumb to their antics and feed one or leave food scraps behind that will attract them.

Past Coffee Bay the trail continues down the shady canal. A variable mixture of Pond Cypress, Loblolly Bay, Sweetbay Magnolia, Titi, Hurrah Bush, and bamboo vine line the wooded banks. At times the broken overstory takes on a scrubby appearance. Belted Kingfishers, hunting the deep water of the canal, often break the quiet seclusion with their rattling call and flashy flight. Watch for Gray Catbirds and American Robins (winter) in the thick shrubs of the canal edge. You also may see an alligator or Florida Cooter (a large aquatic turtle) along the way. Both favor the far edges of the backwater pools.

At mile 7 a vegetation-choked spur canal juts off from the left (west) side of the main canal. Pig Frogs and Florida Cricket Frogs make their home in the thick masses and can be heard calling in season—cricket frogs with their harsh clicking, Pig Frogs with their baritone croaking. Near mile 7.7 the trail narrows to 10 to 15 feet wide as numerous shrubs and trees lean out from the banks and constrict the channel.

Past mile 8, a nice stand of statuesque cypress rises up and borders the canal. Paddling along the colonnade of tall, straight trunks is a treat. Red-shouldered Hawks, Carolina Wrens, Red-bellied Woodpeckers, and Common Yellowthroats add their exuberant voices to the enchanting scene.

At mile 8.9 you reach the junction with the Purple Trail, which leaves the canal from the eastern bank and passes through Chase Prairie on its way to the Round Top overnight shelter.

16 Purple Trail Junction to Canal Run Shelter (Blue Trail Junction)

Distance: 1 mile.
Difficulty: Easy.
Type of trail: Canal.
Hazards: Heat exhaustion, motorboats, airboats, alligators, biting insects.
Habitats: Wooded swamp.
Reliability: Good.
USGS maps: Billys Island-GA, Chase Prairie-GA.
Visitor use: Light to moderate; day-use boating permitted.

See map on page 129

Overview: This short section of the Orange Trail follows the tree- and shrub-lined Suwannee Canal from the Purple Trail junction to the Canal Run shelter. The deep, wide, vegetation-free waters of the canal offer easy and dependable paddling. Wildlife is typical of Okefenokee's woodlands—woodpeckers, hawks, owls, and songbirds. Though open to day-use motorboating, kayaking, and canoeing, few visitors travel this deep into the swamp.

The trail: From mile 8.9 of the Orange Trail, continue north along the Suwannee Canal. The beginning of the Purple Trail leaves the canal on the eastern side. The wooded borders give scant views of Chase Prairie, lying just to the east. Loblolly Bay, Sweetbay Magnolia, Titi, Hurrah Bush, and Wax Myrtle form a thick alley lining the sides of the shady trail. Watch for Wood Ducks, Red-shouldered Hawks, Belted Kingfishers, Gray Catbirds, and Red-bellied Woodpeckers along the canal or in the adjacent forest.

In about 0.5 mile the channel swings to the west. If you take a moment, you can witness the grand miscalculation that lead to Jackson's Folly—the title given to Captain Harry Jackson's doomed attempt to drain the Okefenokee. Jackson's plan was to dredge a canal deep into the heart of the swamp and drain its water into the St. Marys River to the east. One of Jackson's workers, however, made the simple observation some 100 years ago, "If we's aimin' to put the water into the St. Marys, why is it all runnin' toward the Suwannee?" Sure enough, as you look at the water in the canal you notice a slight current flowing not in the direction of the St. Marys, but west toward the Suwannee River.

It's hard to imagine how that realization must have struck Captain Jackson after nearly 10 miles of dredging, years of work, and an extravagant expenditure of money. Though we don't find satisfaction in Jackson's misfortune, we are glad that his plans went awry and the Okefenokee did not come to be just some big muck farm or another timber plantation.

At mile 9.7, you reach the junction with the Blue Trail. The Orange Trail follows the left fork of the canal—the westward extension toward Billys Lake and Stephen C. Foster State Park. The right (northern) fork is the path of the Blue Trail, which crosses the western side of Chase Prairie. From this junction it is only about 0.2 mile down the Orange Trail to the Canal Run overnight shelter. Mature Sweetbay Magnolia, Loblolly Bay, and Wax Myrtle line the canal and spread back into an ever-darkening forest.

The Canal Run shelter sits on the southern side of the trail and is surrounded by a rich woodland of Pond Cypress, Loblolly Bay, Red Maple, Wax Myrtle, Muscadine, Hurrah Bush, Swamp Fetterbush, and Chain Fern. Wood Ducks, Pileated Woodpeckers, Red-shouldered Hawks, Barred Owls, Blue Jays, and White-eyed Vireos call out from the shady depths and whisk by with hardly a fleeting glimpse.

Located on the canal spoil bank, the Canal Run shelter has the added bonus of a little dry land on which you can stretch your legs after the day's paddling. The platform is in good shape, but it is only about 10 feet by 20 feet. You can reasonably expect to pitch only two backpacker-style tents on it; if you have a larger group, you can fit another tent or two on the surrounding dry land.

Fires are permitted, and a fire ring is provided. If you decide to build a fire, plan ahead and pack your firewood in with you (it's only one night's worth). You will save yourself the frustration of trying to find anything dry and avoid marring the charm of the surrounding bay and cypress forest.

17 Canal Run Shelter to Stephen C. Foster State Park

Distance: 7.6 miles.

See map on page 125

Difficulty: Moderate to difficult.
Type of trail: Canal, boat trail.
Hazards: Heat exhaustion, constricted passages, biting and stinging insects, motorboats, airboats, alligators.
Habitats: Wooded swamp, lake.
Reliability: Poor to moderate.
USGS map: Billys Island-GA.
Visitor use: Light to heavy; portions open to day-use boating.

Overview: This section of the Orange Trail is not for the faint of heart, but it makes a great trip for those craving a little wilderness adventure. Beginning at the Canal Run overnight shelter it follows the path of the Suwannee Canal for 1.2 miles before twisting and turning its way along the narrow, contorted channel of the East Fork of the Suwannee River. Low shrubs, downed trees, and mats of floating vegetation can make paddling slow and difficult as you pass through Okefenokee's dense, central forest of bay and cypress. The last 2 miles cross the picturesque Billys Lake on the way to Stephen C. Foster State Park. A variety of woodland birds—woodpeckers, jays, thrushes, wrens, and warblers—can be seen and heard in the shady forest. Alligators, turtles, and the occasional otter add to the trip. Recreational use is light, except on Billys Lake, which can harbor a multitude of swamp visitors. During periods of low water, the trail may become difficult or impassable.

A moment of reflection at the Canal Run shelter.

The trail: After pushing off from the Canal Run shelter, continue west down the Orange Trail following the westward extension of the Suwannee Canal. Okefenokee's dense, central forest of Pond Cypress and bays presses in from every direction. Wax Myrtle, Hurrah Bush, and Swamp Fetterbush lean heavily in from the banks crowding the trail. Robust rafts of vibrant green Hatpins clog the edges—their spiky basal leaf clusters forming dense mats from which the dainty, white, puffy flowers rise on long, needle-thin stalks. Above it all rises the grand swamp forest, arching and curving over the trail. The tallest reaches of the canopy are dominated by Loblolly Bay and Pond Cypress. Underneath grow Red Maple, Sweetbay Magnolia, and hollies.

An ornithologist's ear is helpful in identifying the myriad calls, squawks, and songs emanating from the surrounding forest since the dense growth makes it difficult to see many of the birds that you hear. There are all sorts of sounds—the bright *"cheerie, cheerie, cheerie"* of the Carolina Wren, the screechy calls of the Red-shouldered Hawk, the bizarre buzzes and squeals of the Wood Duck, the harsh, boisterous laughter of the Pileated Woodpecker. Whether or not you can identify them all, the varied sounds enliven the trip.

Other animals are easier to see. Alligators and large, ponderous aquatic turtles haul out on floating logs, rest along the shores, or slowly swim in the quiet waters. Gray Squirrels scamper through the trees, and if you are lucky, you may come upon a family of River Otters hunting their way along the watercourse.

Around mile 10, though still within the Suwannee Canal, you feel more like you are traveling along a lazy river. The straight-sided, orderly nature of the canal is disrupted by overhanging trees and shrubs giving the canal a pleasing, natural aspect as the 10- to 20-foot-wide trail cuts an intimate path through the surrounding forest. Tangled Muscadine vines, thick shrubs, and low trees hang across the trail, at times forming a low canopy. Tight passes alternate with more spacious stretches, leaving you to zigzag your way down the trail. Though the canal usually holds 2 to 3 feet of water, you may encounter sections of the trail partially, or completely, blocked by thick mats of vegetation or fallen trees. Don't be surprised to find yourself struggling to push your way through the blockage or ducking low under the odd deadfall.

Beyond mile 10.2, use of the trail is limited to permit holders and refuge staff, assuring a reasonable measure of solitude on the next 5 miles of your trip. Check the little backwaters that jut off from the sides of the trail for aquatic turtles and other wildlife. In winter, watch for Eastern Phoebes, which prefer to perch over water, in the overhanging branches. This drab flycatcher's conspicuous habit of bobbing its tail makes it easy to identify.

At about mile 11.1 you reach the western end of the Suwannee Canal. Here the trail narrows considerably and becomes a twisting boat trail, 4 to 6 feet wide, that follows the creeklike drainage of the East Fork of the Suwannee River. Under the shady bay forest, a thick undergrowth of Hurrah Bush completely engulfs the trail forming a tunnel-like passage into the forest's gullet. The narrow, twisting

Venturing down narrow, densely vegetated corridors can lead to solitude and discovery.

trail, the encroaching shrubbery, and the obstructing mats of vegetation combine to slow the pace to a tentative stroll at best. Expect to spend twice as long as normal navigating the next 3.5 miles.

At mile 12 the forest thins, creating breaks in the tunnel-like canopy. The added sunlight encourages the growth of some Titi and Poor-man's Soap amid the Hurrah Bush. Along the trail the graceful, arching stems of Swamp Loosestrife rise and fall in low, tangled tussocks. In late summer and fall, the tousled stems are adorned with large, attractive purple blossoms. Hatpins also seem to enjoy the added sunshine and become more prevalent.

For the next 2 miles you will pass in and out of the alternately thickening and thinning melange of forest and shrub. Solo canoeists and kayakers using double paddles may have trouble finding adequate room to dip their blades. Confined tunnel like sections alternate irregularly with scrubby, sun-dappled ones. Fragrant Water Lily, Neverwet, and clumps of Royal Fern with its spectacular, giant fronds dot the understory. Most of the overstory is still comprised of Loblolly Bay, but a few Black Gum, Sweetbay Magnolia, and Pond Cypress assert their presence.

The constricted path of the trail means that you will be scraping and scratching your way through some tight spots. You will probably develop quite a collection of twigs and little spiders in your boat and on yourself as the brittle, dead branches of the shrubs crumble and drop. Many of the spiders are dainty little tetragnathids, which so often spin their webs over water. It only takes a small effort to return them to their homes in the shrubs. A hat with a broad, full brim will help to keep twigs, the beadlike fruits of Titi, spiders, and various other irritating bits from slipping inside your collar and down into your shirt. Also watch out for wasp nests; in particular, there is a small species of paper wasp that likes to build its nest on the undersides of Hurrah Bush leaves. Their sting is quite painful, but the pain is relatively short-lived. The shady, humid environs of the thick shrubs are also attractive to mosquitoes and deer flies. They will be more bothersome here than in more airy places.

At this point you may be thinking that this trail sounds rather unappealing: slow paddling, low shrubs, wasps, spiders. It makes you itch just thinking about it. Well, it's all true, and if you are squeamish about such things you will probably have a more enjoyable time on some other, better-groomed trail. However, if you relish a little adventure and don't mind a good spider in the face now and again, then you may really appreciate this unique paddling experience. There is no other trail in the swamp that will take you so intimately through the dense cypress and bay forest of Okefenokee's interior. Navigating the sometimes cavelike passages will probably be unlike any paddling that you have done before and can be a lot of fun. Along the way White-eyed Vireos, Gray Catbirds, Blue Jays, Pileated Woodpeckers, and Red-shouldered Hawks cavort in the trees, while shy alligators slip away into the dark, obscuring water.

Approaching mile 14 you begin to see patches of open sky above the trail as the character of the surrounding forest begins to change. Pond Cypress replaces

Loblolly Bay as the dominant tree, and the trail loses its tunnel-like character. The shrub thicket relaxes, ceding space to Swamp Loosestrife, Maidencane, yellow-eyed grasses, and wild irises; the latter display their showy, purple blossoms in March and April. Climbing Heath, a small viny shrub related to blueberries, trails up the cypress trunks and over old stumps. Its exquisite, white, bell-shaped flowers are reason enough to take this trip in February and March when they are in bloom.

Soon you pass into an open stand of Pond Cypress. The trail repeatedly widens and narrows, as if in a state of indecision. The wider sections are covered in Spatterdock, and you paddle your way through their robust, floating leaves. The cypress eventually gives way to a scrubby mixture of bays, hollies, Hurrah Bush, and gums.

Near mile 15 you return to the cypress. Be careful to avoid upsetting your boat on the many submerged logs and stumps in this area. They can be difficult to detect in the dark water.

At mile 15.2 you reach the "No Motors/Permit Only" sign and can consider yourself on the skinny, eastern end of Billys Lake (areas west of sign are open to day-use motorboating and canoeing). The trail widens considerably with the increasing expanse of open water. By the time you reach the tip of Billys Island in about 0.1 mile, the lake channel is 35 to 50 feet wide and free of vegetation except along the edges.

Billys Island is one of Okefenokee's high, sandy islands. You may want to stop at the boat dock and take a stroll on the short hiking trail located on the island

A fallen tree presents an obstruction on the Orange Trail.

(secure or carry your valuables). The dry, pine and palmetto uplands of the island are quite different than the woods of the surrounding swamp. Along the trail you see evidence of the island's varied human history, which includes Native Americans, Swampers, and lumbermen. "Artifacts" such as old junk cars and scraps of metal are interspersed with more sacrosanct places, such as burial mounds and a cemetery. The cemetery is fenced off to protect it from intrusion. Sadly, the mounds are not accorded the same measure of protection.

If you stop at Billys Island, be sure not to tarry too long. You will want to have plenty of time to savor the last 2 miles of the trip because Billys Lake is a picturesque gem. The stolid, dark waters of the lake seem to transcend time. Along the shores old, mossy cypresses rise tall and stately—rivaled only by their own reflections. Above, Anhinga flap and soar; Osprey circle and plunge. Below skulk alligators, cooter, Warmouth, and gar.

Located adjacent to Stephen C. Foster State Park, Billys Lake gets more than its fair share of recreational use. Tour boats, sightseers, motorboat operators, anglers, canoeists, and kayakers, all take their turn on the lake. Surrounded by all the natural beauty, though, you will probably not be overly bothered by the buzz of motorboats or increasing bustle of human activity. In fact it is fairly easy to "lose yourself" in some diversion along the shore and completely forget that you may not be alone.

Billys Lake is one of the best places in the Okefenokee to see alligators. In spring and fall, especially, look for them in the many nooks and coves along the shore where they haul out onto logs or peat mats. Please don't get close enough to cause them to retreat into the water. Though lying on a log looks like a lazy and trivial affair, it is actually important work for alligators (and turtles too, for that matter) affecting their metabolism, digestion, and activity level.

Billys Lake is also a good place to see turtles, Pied-billed Grebes (winter), Wood Ducks, White Ibis, Little Blue Herons, and Prothonotary Warblers (summer). Most of the wildlife can be found tucked back in the Spatterdock-covered coves and along the edges of the lake.

Past the island, the lake is lined by a dense forest of Black Gum and Pond Cypress. Spatterdock and Maidencane grow along the edges and occupy occasional openings in the woods. Most of the lake is free of vegetation and generally easy to paddle. However, you should be careful of boat wakes and wind. Sticking close to shore is your best defense for both. If you feel that a motorboat is passing too close or too fast and may swamp your boat with its wake, don't be afraid to signal it to slow down or veer away. Many of the motorboat operators on the lake are inexperienced, and others just may not be paying close enough attention.

At mile 16 you reach the junction with the Red Trail. A beautiful group of mature cypresses stands at the juncture. The lake widens considerably as the Middle Fork of the Suwannee River enters on the north shore. From here, the Red and Orange trails continue west along a common path down the lake toward Stephen C. Foster State Park.

Now about 100 yards wide, the lake is surrounded by large moss-cloaked Pond Cypress, Loblolly Bay, hollies, Sweetbay Magnolia, Titi, and Hurrah Bush. Numerous Spatterdock-covered coves and backwaters dot the shoreline. Most of the lake is free of vegetation, and the open water can get a bit choppy if it is windy. Typically, the lake offers calm and pleasant paddling.

At mile 17.1 you reach the short canal that leads to Stephen C. Foster State Park. The canal enters on the south shore at about the lake's midpoint. It is a wooded, relatively inconspicuous entrance, so watch for the signs that mark it. Follow the gum- and bay-lined canal 0.4 mile to the end of the Orange Trail at the Stephen C. Foster State Park boat basin.

BROWN TRAIL

18 Stephen C. Foster State Park to Cravens Hammock

Distance: 11.2 miles.
Difficulty: Moderate to difficult.
Type of trail: Canal, natural channel, boat trail.
Hazards: Heat exhaustion, biting and stinging insects, constricted passages, lightning, motorboats, alligators.
Habitats: Shrubland, wooded swamp, lake.
Reliability: Poor to moderate.
USGS maps: Billys Island-GA, Cravens Island-GA, The Pocket-GA.
Visitor use: Light to moderate; portions open to day-use boating.

See map on page 130

Overview: This 11.2-mile trail begins at the boat basin of Stephen C. Foster State Park on the western side of the swamp. From the basin the trail takes a path west across Billys Lake, then follows the Suwannee River through a riverine woodland to the Suwannee River Sill, a manmade earthen dam across the Suwannee River. After a jaunt along the sill, it travels north up a scenic, creeklike drainage to the overnight stop at Cravens Hammock. Staying almost entirely within the wooded landscape of a riverine swamp, the trail passes forests of Pond Cypress, Black Gum, Ogeechee Lime, Red Maple, Sweetgum, and hollies. Forest openings and sunny backwaters add variety to the trip. The woodlands are home to Barred Owls, Prothonotary Warblers (summer), Wood Ducks, and Swallow-tailed Kites (summer). Wading birds, particularly White Ibis, can be found foraging in the shallow backwaters. In spring and fall, alligators sun themselves on Billys Lake, on the sill embankment, and along the upper reaches of the creek.

Fluctuating water levels make this the least dependable trip in the swamp. At times the trail is closed due to low water, particularly during fall and early winter. The abundance of submerged logs along the last 5 miles of the trail may require paddlers to exit their boats and lift them over obstacles. With high water and a lightly loaded boat, it is only an minor inconvenience. With low water and a

Counterclockwise from top:
Pond Cypresses reflect in the surface
of Billys Lake, along the Red and
Orange trails; flowering stem of
Meadow Beauty; Sandhill Crane in
Chesser Prairie; Fragrant Water Lily
in bloom along the Green Trail.

PHOTOS BY O'NEILL & O'NEILL

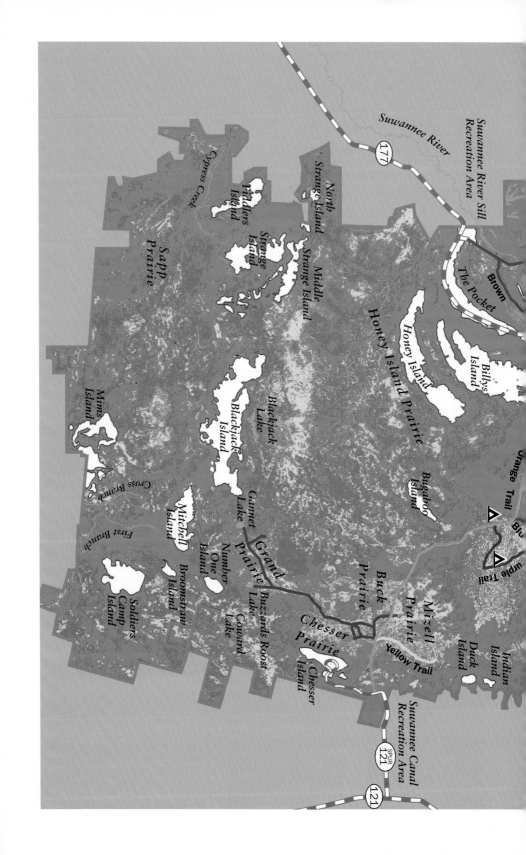

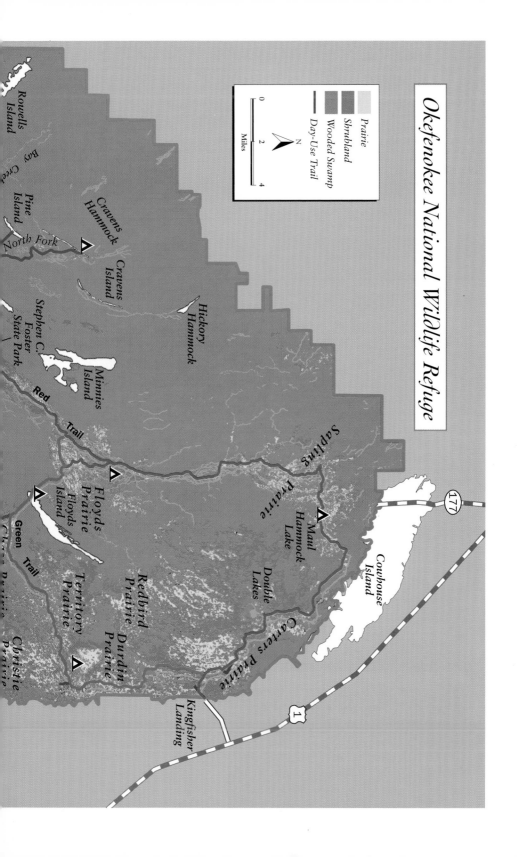

Okefenokee National Wildlife Refuge

Prairie
Shrubland
Wooded Swamp
Day-Use Trail

N

0   2   4
Miles

Rowells Island

Bay Creek

Pine Island

Cravens Hammock

North Fork

Cravens Island

Hickory Hammock

Stephen C. Foster State Park

Mimmies Island

Red

Trail

Sapling Prairie

Maul Hammock Lake

Couhouse Island

177

Floyds Prairie

Floyds Island

Green

Trail

Territory Prairie

Redbird Prairie

Durdin Prairie

Double Lakes

Carters Prairie

Christie Prairie

Chesser Prairie

Kingfisher Landing

1

Counterclockwise from top:
Chesser Prairie at sunset; a young adult
American Alligator cruises Billys Lake;
the flowers and leaves of Saw Palmetto;
and Pine Lily in bloom.

heavily loaded boat, it can be a physical and mental challenge. Be sure to check with refuge personnel about current conditions before you start your trip. Only the last 3.8 miles of the trail are limited to permit holders, therefore you might encounter other swamp visitors (including motorboat operators) along much of the trail. Typically, recreational use is light in these areas and consists mostly of anglers quietly sitting in their boats.

The trail: From the Stephen C. Foster State Park boat basin (a fee is charged), head north up the short 0.4-mile canal that leads to Billys Lake. The 12- to 15-foot-wide canal is lined with a squat, dense mix of Black Gum, Loblolly Bay, Sweetbay Magnolia, Titi, and Hurrah Bush. A few Pond Cypresses rise overhead adding their graceful forms to the scene. Gray Catbirds, Common Yellowthroats, and Pileated Woodpeckers can be often seen.

Upon reaching Billys Lake, turn left (west) and paddle down the lake. The canal enters the lake on the south shore at about its midpoint. Even though it is early in the trip and you might feel the urge to set a brisk pace while you are fresh, take a moment to enjoy the timeless beauty of these dark, cypress-bordered waters.

Billys Lake is a gem. Surrounded by a thick swamp forest, the dark, reflective waters exude a sense of nature primeval. Its charm and accessibility combine to make it a popular spot. Motorboat operators, tour boats, anglers, and day-use paddlers all vie for space on the lake's limited waters. Though never becoming crowded, the lake can be busy on weekends and throughout the months of March and April. Much of this traffic, fortunately, is on the eastern half of the lake,

A Pond Cypress overhangs Billys Lake.

toward Billys Island and the Middle Fork of the Suwannee River and away from the Brown Trail. Still, you should expect to cross paths with other swamp visitors anywhere from the boat basin all the way to mile 7.4.

If you are hoping for a quiet morning on the lake, you can greatly increase your chance of success by scheduling your trip for a weekday and getting on the water as early as possible. If all goes well, your extra efforts will be rewarded.

The western half of Billys Lake is about 100 yards wide and bordered by a thick, somewhat scrubby, forest of Black Gum, Loblolly Bay, and young cypress. Sprinkled about in the mix are a few Swamp Bays, Sweetbay Magnolias, and Red Maples. Titi and Hurrah Bush shrubs comprise the bulk of the understory. At intervals along the shore, large cypresses rise above the dark water in scattered clumps or as lone stragglers. Their grace and beauty give the lake its special character.

The lake's scalloped shoreline harbors numerous nooks and backwaters, which provide sheltered shallows for pockets of Spatterdock and yellow-eyed grasses. By sticking close to shore and skirting the edges of these backwaters you increase your opportunities to see wildlife. You also minimize any trouble with motorboat wakes or wind.

Alligators are common on Billys Lake. In spring and fall, you can easily spot them as they haul out onto logs and shore to warm their bulk in the sun. At the same time you also have a good chance of seeing aquatic turtles following suit. Avoid getting too close and spooking either into the water; sunning is an important part of their ecology.

Billys Lake is also a good place to see birds. Periodically scan the lake for Wood Ducks and Pied-billed Grebes (winter). Search the trees and shrubs along the shore for Common Yellowthroats, Yellow-throated Warblers (summer), Yellow-rumped Warblers (winter), Northern Parulas (summer), White-eyed Vireos, Gray Catbirds, Eastern Phoebes (winter), and Carolina Wrens. Check the backwaters for Great Blue Herons and Great Egrets. Watch for Ospreys and Anhingas soaring above the lake or perching in a tall cypress along the shore. In flight, Ospreys can be recognized at a great distance by the way they hold their wings slightly bent, forming a distinctive crook.

One of the great joys of paddling Billys Lake during the spring and early summer is watching the abundance of Prothonotary Warblers flitting about the cypresses along the lakeshore. Colored in brilliant yellows, golds, and burnished oranges, they flash from branch to branch and sun to shade, brashly singing, "*sweet, sweet, sweet.*"

At mile 1.6 the lake branches into two prongs. Keep to the left (the Brown Trail used to go to the right here) and follow the main route of the Suwannee River southwest toward the Narrows. Past this junction, the lake loses some girth. About 50 yards wide, it is lined by a thick, scrubby forest of Black Gum and Pond Cypress.

At mile 1.8 you reach the end of Billys Lake and see that the lake is really just a wide, slow spot in the river. With seamless transition you glide from the sunny, open water of the lake to the shady channel of the Suwannee River. A varied mix of trees and shrubs quickly encloses the trail, forming an irregular canopy over the river. Black Gum, Pond Cypress, Swamp Bay, Red Maple, and Dahoon Holly occupy the upper layers. Poor-man's Soap, Titi, Virginia Sweetspire, and Hurrah Bush occupy much of the shrubby understory. At odd intervals, small mats of Hatpins and clumps of Maidencane grow with Spatterdock and yellow-eyed grasses along the trail. If water levels are low, be careful of the upright posts of the old logging tram that crosses the river channel at the end of the lake. At high water you will glide right over them without even knowing they are there.

Shortly, you pass the landing at Mixons Hammock. The island and its facilities are reserved for use by groups with special permits. Your destination, Cravens Hammock, lies 9.4 miles farther.

Following in the river channel, the trail is typically 3 to 5 feet deep and 6 to 25 feet wide. The broken forest canopy provides pleasant, shady paddling with enough sun splashes to brighten the way. A few trees and shrubs hang out over the trail now and again, but they are easy to avoid. Overall, the trail passes unconstricted through swamp forest.

Depending on water levels, you will notice a slow to moderate flow (0.5 to 2 miles per hour) in the river. Contrary to what you might expect, the current is usually stronger during low water. This is because there is less of a gradient between the waters of Billys Lake and those backed up by the Suwannee River Sill (located downstream) during high water. Though a welcome aid on the trip in, take note of the current and remember that you will need to overcome it on your return.

Just past Mixons Hammock you enter the Narrows, where the Suwannee River twists and curves over a wide, low rise in the Okefenokee's topography. Water behind the rise pools in Billys Lake. Water flowing over the rise disperses into numerous stream and river channels. The trail follows the main channel, which narrows but remains obvious and easily navigable.

Hopefully by this point you have had a chance to polish up your canoeing skills and have gotten in sync with your partner if you are paddling tandem. Though not challenging, the next 0.7 mile of trail offers some tight curves and unexpected obstacles. Keep an eye out for submerged, or partially submerged, stumps and logs.

As you travel through the Narrows, tight passes between trees alternate with rounded bends and calm backwater pools. Many old cypress stumps stick up along the trail—reminders of the grand cypress forest that once stood here. Always ready to exploit dry footing, many shrubs and trees sprout and grow from these elevated "platforms." One that you are sure to see is a scraggly, little vine called Climbing Heath. Unimpressive throughout much of the year, the little vine is beautifully transformed in February and March when it is decorated with a multitude of delicate, white, bell-shaped flowers.

Overhead, Blue Jays, Red-bellied Woodpeckers, and White-eyed Vireos pass squawking and scolding through the trees. Gray Catbirds and Carolina Wrens call out from deep in the bushes and make their presence known. You may see a few aquatic turtles, but they tend to be skittish—slipping off of their sunning logs and into the river as soon as they spot you.

Gradually the current slows, the curves lessen, and the river gathers back into a single, steady channel. Out of the Narrows the Suwannee once again regains its gentle character. The curvy, 15- to 30-foot-wide trail winds through a thinning forest of Black Gum and Pond Cypress. Spatterdock, yellow-eyed grasses, and Maidencane cover many of the backwaters that crop up along the trail.

By mile 2.8 a broad band of Spatterdock borders each side of the river. Scattered trees, shrubs, and clumps of yellow-eyed grasses and Maidencane dot the watery glades. Conspicuous in their starkness, charred, old cypress stumps jut up in every direction. The fate of many is disguised by decay or the Titi and Virginia Sweetspire shrubs growing on them, but others still display the squared-off tops left by the saw. To either side beyond the Spatterdock, the river channel is lined by a low Black Gum forest.

Now broad and sunny, the river cuts a curving path downstream. Clear of vegetation, it offers relaxed and unimpeded paddling. The Spatterdock glades along the river are a good place to see White Ibis, Little Blue Herons, and Great Egrets. Alligators and Anhingas may also be seen. If water levels are favorable, you might find a Wood Stork. Believe it or not, a Roseate Spoonbill was once spotted along this stretch.

Near mile 3.4 the swamp forest, now a fairly even mix of Black Gum and Pond Cypress, closes in on the river channel. Then in little more than 0.2 mile, the forest abruptly changes. Reminiscent of some mythical forest inhabited by gnomes, the squat, contorted forms of Ogeechee Lime suddenly engulf the trail. Grotesque, and yet hauntingly beautiful, the Ogeechee Lime forest spreads back from the rivercourse in a shadowy thicket. Scattered cypress punctuate the forest, raising their stately trunks skyward in direct contrast to the stunted growth of the limes.

The low trees lining the river provide some shade without obstructing your view of the sky, where Black and Turkey Vultures often soar. Occasionally an Anhinga or two will join them with wings spread and long pointed beak and neck outstretched. Anhingas lack the waterproof feathers typical of most birds, so you often find them perched on a branch overhanging the water with wings spread open toward the sun to dry. If you surprise one as you round a bend, it will drop like lead and crash into the water, disappearing below the surface. Then, 20 or 30 yards downriver, with just its piercing bill and sinewy head and neck visible, it will peer back at you quizzically as it swims away.

At mile 4.6 you reach the Suwannee River Sill. This manmade, 4.6-mile-long earthen dam was authorized by an act of Congress after large fires spread across the swamp and into surrounding areas during droughts in 1954 and 1955. A water-filled ditch parallels the upstream (east) side of the sill. At the sill ditch, turn right and follow it northeast. From the junction you can see the primary water control gates in the sill about 200 yards to the south. There is also a parking lot and boat ramp located 1.5 miles to the left at the southern end of the sill. This area, the Suwannee River Sill Recreation Area, is regularly used by anglers, so you can expect to cross paths with a motorboat or two along the way. The trail follows the sill channel for 1.5 miles before turning up the North Fork of the Suwannee River. Though paddling in a ditch along a dam may sound unappealing, in the more than 35 years that the sill has been in place nature has done its best to reclaim the area.

The eastern side of the sill channel is bordered by broken stands of Black Gum, Ogeechee Lime, and Pond Cypress. Dense woodlands are interrupted by scrubby openings and patches of Spatterdock and Maidencane. To the west of the channel is the low, grassy embankment of the sill. The area behind the sill is drier and holds a mix of Slash Pine, Pond Cypress, Black Gum, Ogeechee Lime, Wax Myrtle, and Red Maple.

The channel itself is about 50 yards wide, 5 to 7 feet deep, and mostly free of vegetation. It is usually calm and easy to paddle, but being linear and somewhat exposed, it can get a little windy at times. It does not provide much protection from sun and rain, so don't forget to break out the sunscreen if you have not already done so.

At times parts of the sill looks like a veritable vulture convention. It's comical to watch them all crowd together at their morning meeting, where they warm themselves in the sun and squabble over important business. The sill area is also a good place to see alligators. They are most conspicuous in spring and fall as they sun themselves along the banks. Watch for them in sheltered, sunny locations at the water's edge. When water levels are low, alligators sometimes congregate in impressive numbers in the deeper water of the sill ditch.

Belted Kingfishers and Ospreys often hunt for fish along the sill. A few herons and egrets may try their luck but usually prefer shallower waters elsewhere. A variety of warblers (Yellow-throated, Northern Parula, Prothonotary, and others) can often be seen among the adjacent trees in the spring. The western side of the sill is a particularly good spot; it is often worth landing your canoe and taking a short walk along the sill to watch and listen for warblers and other birds.

At mile 5.1 the trail takes a bend to the north-northwest, then continues straight along the middle leg of the sill. In another 0.4 mile you reach the secondary water control gates in the sill. The woods on the western side have changed character by this point, now with less pine and more Black Gum, Pond Cypress, and Red Maple. A creek enters on the eastern side about 100 yards north of the sill gates. Continue following the sill channel.

Past the secondary water control gates and the creek, begin watching for the Cravens Hammock sign directing you out of the sill channel and up the Brown Trail. The turnoff is a rather nondescript trail entering on the eastern side of the channel, but it is well marked and easy to find.

Upon reaching the Cravens Hammock sign at mile 6.1, turn right (east) onto the small boat trail that slips into the woods. The 10- to 12-foot-wide trail cuts

Setting up camp on Cravens Hammock.

east through the trees and shrubs for about 75 yards, then intersects another drainage. Turn left (north) at the intersection and continue up the trail.

Now about 20 to 25 feet wide and 5 to 6 feet deep, the trail winds through a scrubby, riverine swamp woodland. Cypress, bays, hollies, maple, Hurrah Bush, and Buttonbush line the trail. Irregular grassy patches of Maidencane occupy openings in the woods. Though called the North Fork of the Suwannee River, you will probably find that the watercourse is more like a creek.

The sluggish river casually weaves its way through the swamp forest. Pileated and Red-bellied Woodpeckers, Red-shouldered Hawks, Gray Catbirds, Great Crested Flycatchers (summer), and Carolina Wrens can be seen and heard in the surrounding woods. Alligators can often be seen in the trail.

Within 0.2 mile you enter a low stand of Black Gum. The variable river channel, though typically 25 to 30 feet wide, broadens at times to 60 feet. A wide grassy fringe of Maidencane lies along much of its border. Mostly free of impeding vegetation and virtually still, the trail remains easy to paddle.

At mile 6.7 the landscape opens up. The woods, now a mix of Black Gum and Pond Cypress, give way to irregular swampy marshes along the sides of the trail. Open and sunny, the marshes attract Wood Ducks, White Ibis, Little Blue Herons, and Great Egrets. Watch for Anhingas and alligators in the deeper water of the river channel. In spring, the area often bustles with activity. Red-shouldered Hawks circle overhead. Pileated and Red-bellied Woodpeckers lope from tree to tree, drumming on this one and that. Little, golden Prothonotary Warblers flash across the trail singing emphatically as they intently investigate each tree cavity for a suitable nest site. And if you are very lucky, a pair of exquisitely graceful Swallow-tailed Kites may silently appear over the woods and sail into view, spread their finely tapered wings and tail, slowly circle and float upwards higher and higher; then swoop down low over the treetops and out of sight. A. C. Bent described the flight of Swallow-tailed Kites as "beautiful in the extreme, unsurpassed in grace and elegance." Anyone fortunate enough to see these beautiful, black-and-white aerial masters at their craft is likely to agree.

Before long, the surrounding cypress and gum woods encroach upon the marshy opening. The trail narrows to a 6- to 10-foot-wide path bordered by a wide fringe of Spatterdock and Maidencane dotted with trees and shrubs. Stillwater pools regularly form within the channel and often harbor hidden stumps and logs, so keep alert. In addition to the Pond Cypress and Black Gum, you will find Red Maple, Buttonbush, Titi and bamboo vine (greenbrier) along the trail. Buttonbush is the tall, robust shrub with long, wrinkled leaves arranged in pairs or whorls. It has unusual, whitish flower heads, which are shaped like little balls.

Be aware that water levels vary considerably along the last 4 miles of the trail. During high water you can expect 2 to 2.5 feet of water in the trail. During the low water typical of fall and early winter, you may have only a foot or less. Even during high water you will occasionally run aground on submerged logs and stumps and possibly have to exit your boat and lift or drag it over the obstacle. At low water, the "bump-stop-drag" routine becomes a regular part of the trip. The trick to low water travel is to pack light in order to keep a shallow draft and consider any obstacles as a fun part of the adventure. Even so, low water travel on the Brown Trail can be slow and physically demanding.

As with anywhere in the Okefenokee, be very careful when exiting your canoe or kayak. Use your paddle to check the water depth and assure firm footing before every step. Along the Brown Trail be especially careful of submerged stumps and logs, which can easily cause you to slip or trip.

At mile 7.4 you reach the "No Motors Beyond This Point. Permit Required" sign. Though you probably have not crossed paths with anyone since leaving the sill, you can be assured of an extra margin of solitude along the rest of the trail. The only people you might encounter are refuge staff, researchers, or the previous canoe party on their way back from Cravens.

At this point the river channel is bordered by a jumbled mix of Maidencane overgrown with Black Gum, Buttonbush, and Titi. Generally more constricted, the trail is typically 5 to 8 feet wide and often clogged with Spatterdock. Within 0.5 mile the trail becomes more twisty. Depending on water levels, you may be able to detect a slight (0.5 to 1 miles per hour) current. The surrounding woods gradually close in, as Black Gum, Dahoon Holly, Titi, and Hurrah Bush crowd the trail. Occasional Spatterdock backwaters dot the way and are good places to find White Ibis, Wood Ducks, Little Blue Herons, and alligators.

Near mile 8, the forest canopy completely engulfs the trail, and you enter a shady shrub thicket of Hurrah Bush, Buttonbush, and Titi. For the next mile the trail jogs west as it traverses a hodgepodge of forest and shrub. The first 0.5 mile pass through a shady Black Gum forest with an understory of Hurrah Bush, Titi, Buttonbush, and Virginia Sweetspire. At times the shrubby understory forms a dense thicket along the trail. Occasional breaks in the canopy provide some sunlight along the way. On the next 0.5 mile, Pond Cypress mingles with the Black Gum, and scrubby openings alternate with shady woods and thickets.

From mile 9 to mile 10 the trail is more open. Irregular stands of cypress and Black Gum are clumped about, but the trail is usually bordered by shrubs and forbs. White Ibis, Great Egrets, and Little Blue Herons often forage in the open shallows. If conditions are favorable, small groups of Wood Storks join them. Belted Kingfishers and alligators can usually be found in the vicinity of deeper pools.

Past mile 10 the 5- to 10-foot-wide, creeklike trail continues twisting and winding through the open mix of trees and shrubs. Tangled banks of Swamp Loosestrife with its arching stems line portions of the trail—their purple blossoms lending a treat for the eyes in late summer and early fall. Increasingly prominent, Maidencane forms grassy swaths along the channel.

At about mile 10.5 the channel widens to 15 to 25 feet in prelude to the small finger lake that lies along the last 0.3 mile of the trail. Admittedly, we are being generous by terming the skinny, 30- to 45-foot-wide body of water a lake, but after the last 3 miles of constricted channel it sure seems like one. The log-choked lake is lined predominately by Pond Cypress and Black Gum. A smattering of Red Maple, Buttonbush, Titi, and Maidencane are also sprinkled about. The lake has a number of coves that allow for a late-afternoon excursion after you have set up camp. In addition to numerous alligators you may find Anhingas, Northern Flickers, Eastern Phoebes (winter), Carolina Wrens, Blue Jays, American Crows, Rusty Blackbirds (winter), and Yellow-throated Warblers (summer).

Continue up the lake following the western shore to the end of the trail where it reaches Cravens Hammock at mile 11.2. A boardwalk and composting toilet extend out from the island at the landing point.

Cravens Hammock is a long, thin island, about 53 acres in size. In the South, the term *hammock* is used to describe certain upland hardwood forests. In this case, the dry, sandy soil of the island supports a rich forest of Live and Water Oaks, Southern Magnolia, and Saw Palmetto, with a few Slash Pine scattered about also.

There is no designated campsite, but the area around the fire ring is pleasant and has a number of suitable tent sites. By using this area, you minimize your impact on the area.

If you poke around a little bit, you will probably find the elevated bed of the old logging tram. It is located west-southwest of the fire ring and makes a great stroll if you have a some spare time in the evening or the next morning. Along the way you are likely to hear or see Pileated Woodpeckers, Carolina Wrens, Tufted Titmice, Wood Thrushes (summer), Gray Catbirds, White-eyed Vireos, and Yellow-rumped Warblers (winter). Gray Squirrels scamper through the trees and chatter their displeasure at your intrusion. As evening approaches, Barred Owls often announce their awaking with a series of throaty calls. You just can't beat a night in the swamp with the air resonating from their rollicking voices.

8. Day Trips

All four access points (see Chapter 6, page 33) listed in this guide offer day-use canoeing and kayaking. Taken together, they provide extensive paddling opportunities and include trails that pass through every major Okefenokee ecotype. The only drawback is that many of the trails open to day-use canoeing are also open to public motorboating. This makes it a bit more difficult to find some wilderness solitude.

SUWANNEE CANAL RECREATION AREA

Trails from the Suwannee Canal Recreation Area extend from the shady tree-lined canal to the extensive open vistas of Mizell, Chesser, and Grand prairies. It is a popular area. Anglers, sightseers, motorboat operators, kayakers, and canoeists flock to these waters. Most of the congestion is restricted to the first 2 miles of the Suwannee Canal. If you hit the water early in the morning, you will avoid most of the traffic. Beyond 2 or 3 miles from the boat ramp in any direction, the number of other boaters greatly diminishes. Wildlife viewing can be excellent. Herons, ibis, Wood Storks, ducks, hawks, and alligators frequent the area. In winter thousands of Sandhill Cranes congregate along the junction of Grand and Chesser prairies and in areas near Gannet Lake. In early spring patches of wildflowers brighten the landscape.

19 Orange Trail

Distance: 10.2 miles; plus additional trails.
Difficulty: Easy.
Start: Suwannee Canal Recreation Area boat ramp.
End: Canal Run Shelter.
Type of trail: Canal.
Hazards: Heat exhaustion, motorboats, airboats, alligators, biting insects.
Habitats: Wooded swamp.
Reliability: Good.
USGS maps: Chesser Island-GA, Chase Prairie-GA, Billys Island-GA.
Visitor use: Moderate to heavy; open to public motorboat use.

See maps on pages 128 and 129

Overview: The first 10.2 miles of the Orange Trail are open to day-use canoeing and kayaking. From the Suwannee Canal Recreation Area boat ramp, the Orange Trail follows the tree- and shrub-lined Suwannee Canal northwest to the Canal Run shelter. Though not the most natural feature of the Okefenokee, the Suwannee Canal offers easy paddling, good wildlife viewing, and nice reflections on the water when the conditions are right. The canal is the main swamp access from the boat ramp to a variety of trails and fishing spots. This makes it a popular and sometimes crowded route. Despite the traffic, it is still a good place to view alligators, aquatic turtles, Anhingas, Great Blue Herons, and Belted Kingfishers. Beyond the first 2 miles of the trail, public use diminishes rapidly. The trail closes only during the most severe droughts.

The trail: Upon leaving the boat ramp (a fee is charged) at the Suwannee Canal Recreation Area, keep to the right (north) as you enter the main channel of the canal and pass the wooded spit along the outgoing traffic route. In addition to staying alert for other boaters, watch for anglers casting their lines from the shores.

The canal was dug by the Suwannee Canal Company in the 1890s in an attempt to drain the Okefenokee for timber and agriculture. After several years of digging and a large expenditure of money, they discovered that the water in the canal was flowing into the swamp, not of out of it. Not surprisingly, they were forced to abandon the project.

The 35- to 40-foot-wide channel of the canal is mostly clear of impeding vegetation and easy to paddle. Since it is 5 to 7 feet deep, only the severest of droughts cause it to become impassable. The sides of the canal are lined by a mix of trees and shrubs. Slash Pine, Pond Cypress, Loblolly Bay, and Dahoon Holly grow over a dense growth of Titi and Hurrah Bush. The clear, dark waters often reflect their images, creating the distinctly Okefenokee ambiance.

A surprising amount of wildlife, including American Alligators, Great Blue Herons, Ospreys, and Anhingas can be found along the canal if you look closely. Watch for many of the animals sitting inconspicuously among the trees and shrubs along the canal margins.

The trail travels west for 1.8 miles to its intersection with the Mizell Prairie day-use trail (Yellow Trail). In another 0.1 mile you reach the Triangle, where an L-shaped leg of the Suwannee Canal splits off from the southern side of the main channel. The two channels eventually rejoin; both are open to day-use boating.

Taking the right fork (northern side of the Triangle), you remain on the Orange Trail and use the most direct route down the canal. The canal narrows to 15 to 20 feet wide, and the trees alongside become a bit scrubbier. There is a composting toilet located on the right (northeast) side of the trail near mile 2.1. At mile 3.1 the southern loop of the Triangle meets the trail again.

The southern side of the Triangle (left fork) leads to the day-use trails in Chesser and Grand prairies. In 0.2 mile from the fork, a large wooden sign marks a boat trail to the south (left); this is the main entrance to Chesser Prairie (and Grand Prairie farther south). You don't have to paddle very far down this trail to get a nice view of Chesser Prairie if you want to take a quick look. Back in the canal you reach another day-use trail in 0.4 mile. This unmarked trail also leaves the canal on the southern side and again leads into Chesser Prairie. Past the second trail, the canal curves to the north and reconnects with the Orange Trail in 0.9 mile. When you reach the junction, you will need to turn left (west) to continue down the Orange Trail.

The Coffee Bay day-use shelter on the Suwannee Canal.

Past the Triangle, the Orange Trail widens to 35 to 40 feet. The sides of the trail are lined with Loblolly Bay, Sweetbay Magnolia, Pond Cypress, Titi, Hurrah Bush, and Wax Myrtle. During the warm months you can expect to see aquatic turtles and an alligator or two, especially if you look carefully into the quiet nooks and backwaters.

The trees and shrubs along the canal are a good place to look for Northern Parulas, Prothonotary Warblers, and Yellow-throated Warblers in the spring and Yellow-rumped Warblers and American Goldfinches in winter. Pileated Woodpeckers, Carolina Wrens, White-eyed Vireos, and Common Yellowthroats can be found year-round. Look carefully at any Anhingas you might see; Double-crested Cormorants look similar and occasionally fish along the canal in winter.

At mile 5.7 you reach the Coffee Bay day-use rest stop where a portion of the southwestern spoil bank has been cleared of undergrowth and outfitted with a covered picnic shelter and composting toilet. Coffee Bay is the small sedge prairie that you can see through the trees to the west. A variety of frogs can be heard calling during the appropriate seasons. The Coffee Bay shelter is a reasonable target destination for the day-use paddler and makes a convenient place to take a paddling break or have lunch before heading back.

Beyond Coffee Bay the trail follows a more northward course. The canal continues through a mix of bays, Pond Cypress, Titi, Hurrah Bush, and Wax Myrtle. In winter you may cross paths with large flocks of American Robins. The woods come alive with their fluttering and chatter as they gobble up the year's berry crop.

At mile 8.9 you reach the junction with the Purple Trail, which enters on the eastern side of the canal. The Purple Trail crosses Chase Prairie and is limited to permit holders and refuge staff.

In another 0.8 mile you reach the junction with the Blue Trail. The Blue Trail follows the right (north) fork of the canal for 0.4 mile, then meanders in and out of Chase Prairie for 2.2 miles along a winding boat trail. Most of the Blue Trail is open to day-use boating and allows access to Chase Prairie, though only the fastest and most fit paddlers are likely to complete the 24.2-mile round trip in a day.

The Orange Trail follows the left (west) fork of the canal and is open to day-use paddling to mile 10.2. The canal is heavily wooded as it passes into the dense swamp forest of the Okefenokee's interior. Loblolly Bay, Pond Cypress, Red Maple, Sweetbay Magnolia, Titi, Hurrah Bush, and Swamp Fetterbush lean out from the canal banks and close over the trail.

The Canal Run shelter is located on the southern bank of the Orange Trail at mile 9.9 and is surrounded by a lush woodland. It is used as one of the campsites on the designated overnight canoe trips and has a covered platform, composting toilet, and small bit of dry land on which to walk around. It is open to day-use, but the 19.8-mile round trip will leave it beyond the of reach of most paddlers. If you make it to the Canal Run shelter and a permitted canoe trip group arrives, please be courteous and respect their privacy.

20 Yellow Trail

Distance: 3 miles.
Difficulty: Moderate.
Start: Orange Trail mile 1.8.
End: Mizell Prairie.
Type of trail: Boat trail.
Hazards: Heat exhaustion, lightning, peat quagmires, airboats, alligators, biting insects.
Habitats: Prairie, shrubland, wooded swamp.
Reliability: Good.
USGS maps: Chesser Island-GA, Chase Prairie-GA.
Visitor use: Light to moderate; public access limited to day-use canoeists.

See map on page 131

Overview: From the Suwannee Canal, the Yellow Trail follows a serpentine course northward through the patchwork of prairie, shrub, and wood of Mizell Prairie. It is the first trail off the canal and therefore appealing to those with limited time. It takes you through a variety of swamp ecotypes and provides good wildlife viewing opportunities. White Ibis, Little Blue Herons, Sandhill Cranes, and numerous frogs frequent the prairie sections. Songbirds and Wood Ducks are common in the shrubby areas. Red-shouldered Hawks and Barred Owls hunt from the numerous cypress stands. Being limited to day-use canoeists and kayakers, it is a good place to enjoy the Okefenokee away from the hum of motorboats. Prolonged droughts sometimes cause the trail to be closed.

The trail: To reach the trail, follow the Orange Trail (Suwannee Canal) west for 1.8 miles from the Suwannee Canal Recreation Area boat ramp (a fee is charged).

101

The Yellow Trail begins on the northern side of the canal, just before you reach the Triangle.

From the shady, tree-lined canal, the Yellow Trail enters the sunny sedge glades and water lily marshes of Mizell Prairie. The trail makes a sweeping arc to the west, passing a dense cypress stand, before taking a predominantly northward course.

Mizell Prairie's multitude of young cypress domes are surrounded by the freeform growth of the intervening sedges, grasses, and shallow water lily pools. Walter's Sedge, beakrushes, yellow-eyed grasses, Redroot, Fragrant Water Lily, and Neverwet crowd the openings between tidy stands of Pond Cypress and Hurrah Bush. The airy combination provides a continual series of views, which unfold as you cross the prairie.

Keep a sharp lookout for Sandhill Cranes. With their keen eyesight they will most likely spot you first and then endeavor to blend unnoticed into the prairie landscape. Sometimes they protest your presence with their gravelly trumpeting.

Past mile 1, the 5- to 10-foot-wide boat trail curves to the northeast. The adjacent marshes are frequented by White Ibis, Great Egrets, Little Blue Herons, and Wood Ducks. In fall and winter, you may scare up some Blue-winged or Green-winged Teals—their rapid wingbeats taking the compact flock careening across the horizon.

At just about any time of year, you can see an abundance of little Florida Cricket Frogs and listen to their clacking calls emanating from the surrounding marsh. In spring, Pig Frogs add their guttural croaking and Carpenter Frogs

White Ibis forage in Mizell Prairie.

hammer out their unusual song—a combination of knocks and echoes that sound like someone pounding nails into the two-by-four framework of a new house.

From mile 2 to mile 3, the trail swings back to the north. Gradually the vegetation thickens, as sedges and cypress give way to Titi, yellow-eyed grasses, and Loblolly Bay. In the increasing trees and shrubs you can find Common Yellowthroats, Swamp Sparrows (winter), and Gray Catbirds. The Yellow Trail is not open to travel beyond mile 3.

21 Day-Use Trails in Chesser and Grand Prairies

Distance: 7.6 miles; plus additional trails.
Difficulty: Moderate.
Start: Southern Side of Suwannee Canal Triangle.
End: Gannet Lake.
Type of trail: Boat trail.
Hazards: Heat exhaustion, lightning, motorboats, airboats, alligators, biting insects.
Habitats: Prairie, wooded swamp.
Reliability: Moderate to good.
USGS map: Chesser Island-GA.
Visitor use: Moderate to heavy; portions open to public motorboat use.

See map on page 131

Overview: Beginning at the entrance to Chesser Prairie, these popular trails traverse south through two wildlife-rich prairies. Watch for alligators, frogs, herons, hawks, cranes, ducks, and more as you paddle across the watery plain. The prairies are also a good place to see a variety of wildflowers, especially in late winter and early spring when Hatpins, Neverwet, and bladderworts are in bloom. A number of short side trips and alternate routes are possible by traveling the network of interconnecting trails. Chesser Prairie is a popular destination. Visitor use on the first couple of miles of trail is typically moderate but diminishes farther from the trailhead. The trails occasionally close due to drought.

The trails: To reach the trails, follow the Orange Trail (Suwannee Canal) west for 1.9 miles from the Suwannee Canal Recreation Area boat ramp (a fee is charged). Then take the left fork of the canal (southern side of the Triangle) toward Chesser Prairie. The trail begins on the southern (left) side of the canal 0.2 mile beyond the fork.

Leaving the canal and entering Chesser Prairie you are greeted by a different world. Here the forest of pine, bays, and cypress opens to reveal extensive prairies of Fragrant Water Lily, Neverwet, and a variety of sedges and grasses. Cypress trees and Titi shrubs form small wooded islets and groves, which sit amid the prairie. The wide, easy-to-paddle trail travels south through Chesser Prairie and provides excellent views of both wildlife and scenery.

Maidencane, in foreground, borders the day-use trails in Chesser and Grand prairies.

At 0.4 mile from the canal, the trail forks. The left (east) fork is limited to canoe and kayak travel and leads 0.3 mile to the generously named Cooter Lake. While you are not likely to find any cooters or even much of a lake, this is a much less used section of trail and just as scenic.

The right (west) fork of the trail continues through Chesser Prairie toward Grand Prairie. Scattered clumps of mature cypress and numerous dead standing trees support the bulky stick nests of Great Blue Herons. In this part of the prairie the numerous tree-islands are well defined and separated by open prairie. Yellow-eyed grasses and Redroot grow along the trail. Wildlife viewing can be very rewarding with the possibilities including alligators, Anhinga, Wood Duck, Great Egret, Sandhill Crane, and Red-shouldered Hawk.

At mile 1 you intersect a secondary trail. The trail to the right (west) crosses a wooded mix of prairie for 0.8 mile and reconnects with the Triangle on the Suwannee Canal. The 0.6-mile trail to the left (east) crosses water lily pools and sedge meadows on its way to the previously mentioned Cooter Lake (see above), and is limited to canoe and kayak travel.

Continuing straight, the trail narrows slightly and becomes a gently winding, 6-to 10-foot-wide boat trail. Along the eastern side, broad isolated water lily pools weave through the thickening cypress. Scattered shrubs and swaths of yellow-eyed grasses, sedges, and Maidencane fringe the islands and rim the prairie pools. The western side is more wooded. Low, sprawling shrub-islands, clumps of cypress, and Loblolly Bay surround scattered prairie pockets.

Past mile 2 the amount of open prairie diminishes steadily as you paddle toward the southern limit of Chesser Prairie. At mile 3 the trail passes into the forest of cypress, pine, and bays that separates Chesser and Grand prairies. The wooded prairies on either side of this forest can be filled with hundreds of Sandhill Cranes during the winter months. Unlike the year-round residents, these migrants often associate in flocks of 20 or more and make a dramatic image as they fly over the prairie.

In approximately 0.7 mile you enter Grand Prairie, another expansive open wetland. Most of Grand Prairie is comprised of sedges, yellow-eyed grasses, Maidencane, and Broomsedge marshes, which wrap around scattered groves of Pond Cypress and Titi. There is also a substantial amount of shallow open-water prairie with Neverwet, Fragrant Water Lily, and Arrow Arum. The trail traverses Grand Prairie for 4 miles and provides wonderful touring. American Alligators, Wood Ducks, Green-winged and Blue-winged Teals (winter), Great Egrets, Little Blue Herons, Sandhill Cranes, and White Ibis can be found.

At mile 4.3, a short 0.1-mile spur trail leaves the main path on the right (west) and goes to Little Cooter Lake.

At mile 4.7 the trail forks. The left (east) fork follows a 0.7-mile spur trail directly south to two lakes. Starting in the open prairie, the spur soon becomes more wooded as Swamp Bay, Sweetbay Magnolia, Dahoon Holly, Titi, and Swamp Fetterbush crowd out the prairie. In 0.3 mile you reach Monkey Lake, a small grass-fringed lake surrounded by shrubs and trees. A day-use rest shelter with composting toilet sits in the shady woods on the southern side of the lake. On cool mornings, numerous Green Anoles (small lizards) clamber out from the nearby shrubs and warm themselves on the exposed portions of the platform. Past Monkey Lake the trail crosses a scrubby mix of shrubs, low trees, and grasses. At the end of the spur trail, you reach Buzzards Roost Lake. The 17-acre lake is ringed by a line of low shrubs and is very scenic. Maidencane and Swamp Loosestrife fringe the shallow margins.

Back on the main trail, the right (west) fork veers to the southwest and continues across the sweeping, open vistas of Grand Prairie. White Ibis, Great Egrets, and Little Blue Herons can often be seen hunting in the extensive marshes. In winter, Sandhill Cranes, Wood Ducks and teal sometimes gather in large numbers along the wooded margins. On some days, flock after flock can be seen passing along the horizon.

In about 1 mile you reach Goose House Gap, where the forest temporarily converges on the prairie. Cypress, bays, and pines close in from either side, and the trail becomes shrubby and wooded.

Past the gap, a short respite from the swamp forest allows the recurrence of prairie openings. Fragrant Water Lily, Neverwet, yellow-eyed grasses, and Maidencane grow in meandering patches and broad pools bordered by Pond Cypress and Loblolly Bay. The prairie respite is short lived, and within 0.5 mile the trail becomes shrubby and wooded again.

At mile 6.7, another spur trail from the right (north). The 0.9-mile trail leads along a shrubby path to two very small lakes, one of two pairs of lakes in the Okefenokee called Double Lakes.

The main trail continues to the southwest and becomes increasingly wooded. Eventually you pass into a wooded tunnel where the contorted trail passes through a dense thicket. On the far side of the thicket you will reach Gannet Lake (mile 7.4). The open water of the lake is bordered by shrubs on three sides. The western side has a nice fringe of yellow-eyed grasses and sedges. Though few waterfowl visit, you can usually find an alligator somewhere around the lake. It is a pleasant lake (about 500 yards wide), but really farther than you can hope to get to and back in a day's paddle.

KINGFISHER LANDING

Kingfisher Landing provides access to the shrubby, wooded sections of the Red Trail, the open prairie vistas of the Green Trail, and wide tannin-stained waters of the Kingfisher canals. A few anglers motor these waters on a regular basis, but overall, Kingfisher Landing is the least used access point.

22 Red Trail

Distance: 5.1 miles; plus additional trails.   See map on page 122
Difficulty: Moderate to difficult.
Start: Kingfisher Landing.
End: Double Lakes.
Type of trail: Canal, boat trail.
Hazards: Peat quagmires, lightning, heat exhaustion, motorboats, airboats, biting insects.
Habitats: Shrubland, wooded swamp, lake.
Reliability: Good.
USGS map: Double Lakes-GA.
Visitor use: Light to moderate; open to public motorboat use.

Overview: The first 5.1 miles of the Red Trail are open to day-use canoeing (and motorboating) and provide intimate touring through the extensive shrublands typical of this part of the swamp. The trail begins at Kingfisher Landing and travels northwest through a mix of shrub and small prairie openings to Double Lakes. Although not one of the best wildlife viewing areas, there always seems to be something around to enliven the trip. The Red Trail is one of the least used day-use boating areas. Water levels are usually sufficient for paddling, and the trail only occasionally closes due to drought.

The trail: The trail begins by following the path of the 40- to 50-foot-wide canal from the landing. The spoil banks of the canal are lined with a variety of trees and shrubs: Slash Pine, Loblolly Bay, Dahoon Holly, Titi, Hurrah Bush, Swamp Fetterbush, and Wax Myrtle. If the water is calm, they reflect beautifully on the dark waters. In fall and winter the red berries of Dahoon Holly are particularly attractive.

Follow the canal past the Green Trail/Bluff Lake turnoff at mile 1, remaining on the Red Trail. Near the end of the canal (mile 1.6) the trail veers off to the northwest (left) and becomes a 5- to 10-foot-wide, winding boat trail. Here the trail passes a varied combination of cypress, pine, shrub, and prairie. Small pools of Fragrant Water Lily, swaths of yellow-eyed grasses, patches of sedges, clumps of shrubs, and stands of Pond Cypress intermingle within the scrambled hodgepodge. Common Yellowthroats, Northern Mockingbirds, Swamp Sparrows (winter), and Eastern Phoebes (winter) are commonly seen.

For those interested in a little diversion, a spur trail loops off the northeastern side of the main trail at mile 1.8. The 0.5-mile spur goes to tiny Trout Lake. Though eventually rejoining the Red Trail at mile 2.2, the last portions of the spur are overgrown and difficult to travel.

Along the main trail, the shrubs become increasingly prevalent. Titi, Swamp Fetterbush, and Hurrah Bush grow along the trail and permeate the adjacent prairie. Broomsedge, yellow-eyed grasses, Maidencane, and Fragrant Water Lily are relegated to thin strips and small pockets. Pond Cypresses weave through the shrubby mix in irregular bands and isolated stands.

Between mile 3 and mile 4 the trail is more wooded as Pond Cypress, Hurrah Bush, and Titi crowd out the diminishing prairie. Small openings in the shrubby forest still hold occasional pockets of sedges, yellow-eyed grasses, and Broomsedge, and in the nooks and margins you can find clumps of Hooded Pitcher Plant and tufts of Hatpins. Watch for Pileated and Red-bellied Woodpeckers, Northern Flickers, Eastern Phoebes (winter), Carolina Wrens, and Red-shouldered Hawks.

Past mile 4 the trail is lined by a shrubby corridor of Titi, Swamp Fetterbush, Hurrah Bush, and bamboo vines. Though the thick shrubs restrict your view to little more than the trail, they offer calm paddling on a windy day and allow close observation of one of the Okefenokee's major habitats. Wood Ducks frequently rest along the trail, taking flight as you paddle around a bend and startle them. Gray Catbirds and a variety of other birds seek shelter in the dense shrubs and regularly flit back and forth across the trail.

Near mile 4.5 the shrubs thin and make room for scattered Pond Cypress and pines. At mile 4.8 you reach the small prairie adjacent to Double Lakes. Shrub-dotted glades of yellow-eyed grasses and sedges fill the opening of Carters Prairie to the north. Pockets of Fragrant Water Lily and stands of Pond Cypress accent the landscape.

At mile 4.9 there is a 0.2-mile spur trail to the left (west-southwest), which leads to the first of the Double Lakes. The 17-acre lake is surrounded by a low growth of trees and shrubs. Much of the lake is free of vegetation and easy to explore. The southeastern margin holds a wide fringe of Spatterdock and is worth investigating. You can sometimes find Anhingas, Blue-winged and Green-winged Teals (winter), Pig Frogs, and alligators.

As a day-use paddler, you are only permitted about 0.1 mile past Double Lakes on the Red Trail. The short jaunt past the lake does, however, provide additional views of the surrounding prairie.

23 Green Trail

Distance: 7.6 miles; plus additional trails.
Difficulty: Moderate.
Start: Kingfisher Landing.
End: Bluff Lake shelter.
Type of trail: Canal, boat trail.
Hazards: Peat quagmires, lightning, heat exhaustion, motorboats, airboats, biting insects.
Habitats: Prairie, shrubland, wood swamp, lake.
Reliability: Good.
USGS maps: Double Lakes-GA, Chase Prairie-GA.
Visitor use: Light to moderate; open to public motorboat use.

See map on page 126

Overview: From Kingfisher Landing you can paddle the first 7.6 miles of the Green Trail to the Bluff Lake shelter. The trail heads south along the eastern edge of the Okefenokee through the sedge glades and cypress domes of Durdin Prairie. The boggy marshes hold a diversity of plants and wildlife. Watch for pitcher plants, Hatpins, Grass Pinks, Carpenter Frogs, Florida Cricket Frogs, Great Egrets, and Tree Swallows (winter). Few people venture beyond the canals, so you can expect to have much of Durdin Prairie to yourself. Only the most severe droughts cause the trail to become impassable.

The trail: Beginning at the boat ramp, follow the wooded canal for 1 mile. Then turn left (southwest) at the Green Trail/Bluff Lake turnoff. In 0.5 mile the canal splits into two parallel channels. The Green Trail follows the right (west) canal, but both are equally canoeable. You might try one on the way out and the other on the way back.

At mile 1.9 the trail makes a short jog to the right (west) as two spur canals enter the trail from the eastern side. Both of these spurs are also open to day-use canoeing if you are in the mood to explore them. To continue along the Green Trail, just follow the jog around and keep heading south. It is not as confusing as it sounds. As long as you keep to the west after making the initial turn at mile 1, you should stay on track (see map inset, page 126).

At mile 2.4 the trail leaves the canal and enters Durdin Prairie. For the next 5.2 miles you pass sweeping glades of sedges and Maidencane, scattered stands of Pond Cypress, and sprawling clumps of Titi, Hurrah Bush, and Swamp Fetterbush. Durdin Prairie has something for just about everyone. For the ornithologist there are Wood Ducks, Great Egrets, Sandhill Cranes, Red-shouldered Hawks, Great Crested Flycatchers (summer), and Common Yellowthroats. For the herpetologist there are alligators, Florida Cooters, and more frogs than you can count. For the botanist there are Grass Pinks, Parrot Pitcher Plants, Hatpins, Arrow Arum, and Narrow-leaved Sundews. Add the beautiful scenery, and you have the ingredients for a great day's paddle.

At mile 4.3 you cross the very small, Spatterdock-covered Flag Lake and wonder why anyone bothered naming it. Past Flag Lake, the winding, 6- to 10-foot-wide boat trail continues through a mix of low sprawling shrub-islands and sedge mead-ows. Small cypress stands and water lily pools are liberally sprinkled throughout the shrubs and sedges.

At mile 6.5 you reach Durdin Lake. Though the short jaunt around the 12-acre lake is not likely to reveal much wildlife, it is a pleasant detour.

In about another mile, you reach Bluff Lake. This open-water lake is rimmed by a thick growth of Titi and Hurrah Bush. The Bluff Lake shelter sits about 0.1 mile west of the lake along the Green Trail (mile 7.6). The shelter is a good place to take a break from paddling and has a composting toilet. It is one of the campsites for the overnight canoe trips. If you happen upon a permitted canoe party at the shelter, be courteous and minimize your intrusion.

Beyond the shelter day-use boating is permitted only for about another 0.2 mile, where the trail passes into the shrubby, western edge of Durdin Prairie. If you find yourself with some extra time, consider paddling the unmarked, day-use trail to Half Moon Lake. The trail starts from the southeastern shore of Bluff Lake—just south of where the Green Trail enters the lake on the eastern side. From there, the trail travels 0.3 mile to Half Moon Lake, home to an abundance of Pig Frogs and Florida Cricket Frogs.

SUWANNEE RIVER SILL RECREATION AREA

It may seem contradictory, but the Okefenokee Swamp is naturally prone to drought and fire. In 1954 and 1955 the droughts were particularly severe, and fires swept across much of the swamp. Whereas the swamp ecosystem is adapted to, even dependent on, such occurrences, most people in the surrounding area are not. In response, a 4.6-mile-long, earthen dam was built across the main outflow of the swamp, the Suwannee River, in an attempt to control fire and erosion. The Suwannee River Sill, as it is called, stretches northward from the western end of The Pocket to Pine Island. The waterway along the sill is open to day-use boating and pro-vides access to the riverine swamps characteristic of the Suwannee River drainage.

24 Suwannee River Sill Day-Use Trails

Distance: 4.6 miles; plus additional trails. *See map on page 130*
Difficulty: Easy.
Start: Suwannee River Sill Recreation Area boat ramp.
End: Pine Island.
Type of trail: Canal.
Hazards: Heat exhaustion, lightning, motorboats, alligators, biting insects
Habitats: Wooded swamp.
Reliability: Moderate to good.
USGS map: The Pocket-GA.
Visitor use: Moderate; open to public motorboat use.

Overview: Paralleling the upstream (east) side of the Suwannee River Sill is a 50-yard-wide, canoeable waterway (actually the ditch from which they removed soil to build the dam). The wide, clear trail passes wooded swamps of Pond Cypress, Black Gum, Ogeechee Lime, Red Maple, and Slash Pine. Scrubby openings and backwaters hold patches of Maidencane, Titi, Redroot, and Spatterdock. The woods are host to Barred Owls, Wood Ducks, Swallow-tailed Kites (summer), Prothonotary Warblers (summer), and a variety of woodpeckers. Alligators have adapted well to the intrusion of the sill and often use it for basking in the spring and fall. In addition to paddling the sill channel, a couple of side trips are available. The area is popular with local anglers, but motorboat traffic is usually moderate. As part of the of the fluctuating waters of the Suwannee River drainage, the trail sometimes closes due to drought.

The trail: From the boat ramp paddle northeast along the sill. For its entire length the channel is wide and easy to paddle. The eastern side is bordered by young stands of Black Gum and Pond Cypress. Openings filled with Spatterdock and Redroot intermingle with the forest.

The western side of the channel is bordered by the grassy embankment of the sill. A marshy fringe of Maidencane and Spatterdock grows along the western edge, but most of the channel is free of vegetation. Parents with fidgety children (or children with fidgety parents for that matter) will appreciate being able to land the canoe anywhere along the sill bank for a paddling break. Just be careful of Fire Ant colonies.

The woods to the west behind the sill are much drier and very different from those to the east. The overstory is a mix of Slash Pine, Pond Cypress, and Red Maple. In the understory is Wax Myrtle, Swamp Bay, and Black Gum. In spring, these woods are a good place to see a variety of warblers, including Yellow-rumped, Yellow-throated, Prothonotary, and Northern Parula.

Just before mile 1.5 you reach the main water control gates of the Suwannee River Sill. The large cypresses in this area are a favorite roost of Black and Turkey Vultures. If you pull up to the shore and scan the downstream side of the gates, you may see Great Egrets, Little Blue Herons, or Great Blue Herons fishing along the banks.

About 200 yards farther, the Suwannee River enters on the eastern side of the ditch. Even if you don't follow it all the way to Billys Lake (2.8 miles), it is still worth taking a quick peek up this famous river. Paddling up the river through the Ogeechee Lime thicket is like entering one of the mangrove forests in the Everglades. The Suwannee River is the path of the Brown Trail, and at the sill the Brown Trail turns north and follows the sill for 1.5 miles.

Continuing up the sill channel, the woods on the eastern side become thick and scrubby. Black Gum, Ogeechee Lime, and Pond Cypress crowd together in dense stands. The few shrubby openings are filled with Titi and Maidencane. White Ibis, Belted Kingfishers, Great Crested Flycatchers (summer), and Red-bellied Woodpeckers are commonly seen.

The day-use trail in the Suwannee River Sill Recreation Area.

At mile 2.0 the sill makes a bend to the left and heads north-northwest. By this point you have left most of the public behind. With less human activity you are more likely to see a Raccoon, a White-tailed Deer, or even a Black Bear meandering along the sill.

In 0.4 mile you reach the second set of water control gates. The woods on the western side have changed character, now being comprised mostly of Black Gum, Pond Cypress, and Red Maple. As with the first set of gates, it is worth landing your canoe and looking around. In addition to Little Blue Herons and Great Egrets, a number of large alligators frequent the area. In the spring, you can sometimes see three or four "big ones" sunning on the bank—an impressive sight.

At mile 3.0 the Brown Trail leaves the sill and follows the North Fork of the Suwannee River to Cravens Hammock. The first 1.3 miles from the sill are open to day-use boating and make a nice change of pace for those interested in a side trip. You wind along the creeklike river channel through swamp forest for 0.6 mile before entering a marshy opening where Maidencane and Spatterdock backwaters border the rivercourse. The area can be great for wildlife viewing, especially in spring.

The sill channel continues north-northwest past the Brown Trail junction for 0.2 mile, then makes a final bend to the northwest. From the bend it is another 1.4 miles to the end of the sill at Pine Island. The woods along the eastern side of the channel grow in stature and develop a dense shrub understory. The western woods remain a hodgepodge of Pond Cypress, Black Gum, and Red Maple. Among them you can also find Wax Myrtle, hollies, Titi, and Hurrah Bush. If you decide to paddle all the way to the end of the sill you may be rewarded by seeing a pair of Hooded Mergansers (winter) or Wood Ducks, which prefer the quiet seclusion found there.

STEPHEN C. FOSTER STATE PARK

From Stephen C. Foster State Park you can paddle along the picturesque shores of Billys Lake and wander through stately groves of Pond Cypress. You can trek the thick gum forests of the lower swamp or explore the upper reaches of the Suwannee River. Certainly one of the most famous features of the Okefenokee, the Suwannee River seems to capture all that is meant by the phrase "Old Man River." Grand, subtle, vibrant, quiet, lazy, and insistent, the Suwannee is born from a myriad of tributaries that form, disperse, and reform in the swampy landscape of the Okefenokee.

25 Red Trail

Distance: 10.8 miles.
Difficulty: Moderate.
Start: Stephen C. Foster State Park boat ramp.
End: Big Water Lake.
Type of trail: Canal, natural channel.
Hazards: Motorboats, airboats, alligators, biting insects.
Habitats: Wooded swamp, lake.
Reliability: Moderate.
USGS maps: Billys Island-GA, Dinner Pond-GA.
Visitor use: Moderate to heavy; open to public motorboat use.

See maps on pages 123 and 125

Overview: From Stephen C. Foster State Park you can travel 10.8 miles up the Red Trail to the top of Big Water Lake. The trail travels east across Billys Lake, then follows the Middle Fork of the Suwannee River northeast through a shady swamp forest to Big Water Lake. Though the entire trip is more than most paddlers would want to attempt in a day, any portion offers wonderful scenery and pleasant paddling. Alligators, Ospreys, White Ibis, Little Blue Herons, and a variety of woodland birds frequent the area. The area is popular with sightseers and anglers alike. Finding a secluded spot may not always be the easiest thing to do, but the beautiful scenery should more than make up for it. Being susceptible to drought, portions of the trail are sometimes closed due to low water.

The trail: Note that from Stephen C. Foster State Park, you will be starting at the end of the Red Trail. This just means that the Red Trail mile figures are based on the distance from Kingfisher Landing, not Stephen Foster. For instance, the boat ramp where you will be starting is Red Trail mile 31.8.

Follow the short 0.4-mile canal north from the boat ramp (a fee is charged) to Billys Lake. At the lake, turn right (east) and follow the lake. Billys Lake is about 100 yards wide and lies in an ancient depression in the sandy floor of the swamp. The lake is one of the most scenic features of the Okefenokee. With changing light, season, and atmosphere it harbors a thousand moods.

A thick forest of Loblolly Bay, Sweetbay Magnolia, Black Gum, hollies, Titi, and Hurrah Bush surrounds the lake. Along the shores grand, mossy Pond

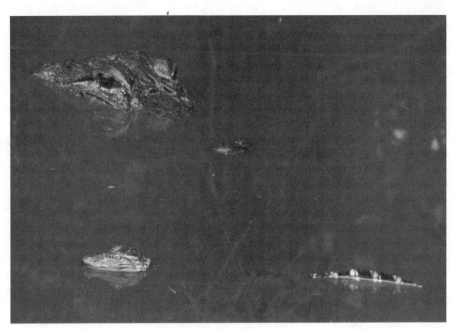

A mother alligator keeps a close eye on her young.

Cypress rise above the dark waters and cast wonderful reflections on the lake in the calm of morning and evening. An irregular fringe of Spatterdock rims the lake and covers numerous backwater coves.

Many alligators and aquatic turtles make their home on Billys Lake. In spring and fall you can spot them in sunny locations on the banks. During summer the water is warm enough that they stop sunning on the banks, and you may have to be content with seeing just their heads poking above the water surface. Billys Lake is also a good place to look for birds. Scan the Spatterdock-covered coves for White Ibis and Little Blue Herons. Check the tallest cypresses for Ospreys and Anhingas, and search the woods along the shore for a variety of warblers.

After 1.1 miles across the lake you reach the inlet of the Middle Fork of the Suwannee River on the north shore (Red Trail mile 30.3). Turn left and follow the river upstream toward Minnies Lake. Currents in the river channel are typically 2 miles per hour or less and generally do not pose a difficulty.

Leaving the lake, the river passes into a shady, mixed-age cypress forest. Venerable, broad-trunked old-timers form a patchwork with scrubby, dense stands of adolescents. Black Gum, Swamp Bay, hollies, Titi, and Hurrah Bush grow in the understory and amid gaps in the canopy.

Averaging 25 to 60 feet wide, the gently curving river narrows and widens as it squeezes between trees and spreads out around lazy bends. Irregular patches of Spatterdock, yellow-eyed grasses, and Maidencane grow along the calm edges and backwaters of the channel. Watch for White-tailed Deer, American Alligators, Wood Ducks, and White Ibis along the shores and in the adjacent woods.

In about 1 mile the trail narrows and becomes more twisting as you weave your way around the bulbous bases of the encroaching cypresses. Over the next 0.5 mile you get some of the most intimate views of mature cypress in the swamp. The beauty of these graceful trees is beyond words. After passing through the middle of the cypress grove, the trail regains its gently curving nature.

About 3.4 miles from the boat ramp (Red Trail mile 28.4) you reach the southern end of the 1.1-mile-long Minnies Lake, which is little more than a wide, slow stretch of the river. A small day-use rest shelter is located at the south end of the lake. The covered platform sits in the shady woods on the northwestern side of the trail and makes a convenient place to take a paddling break. It is not equipped with a toilet.

The long, narrow lake is surrounded by an attractive cypress forest. The shady lower half has a shrubby Titi and Hurrah Bush border. The sunny upper half is a little broader, and all but the central channel is covered with a thick growth of Spatterdock.

Above Minnies Lake, the trail narrows to 10 to 25 feet wide. Maidencane, yellow-eyed grasses, and Spatterdock grow in irregular patches alongside the central channel. Be careful: Submerged logs and stumps can snag your boat at low water.

For the next mile you pass through a scrubby mix of Pond Cypress and Black Gum. A dense undergrowth of Titi and Hurrah Bush form shrub corridors and crowd portions of the trail. Scattered stands of mature cypress grow throughout the area. At one point you pass directly through one of the cypress stands and get another chance to view these beautiful trees close-up as you navigate around their sweeping trunks.

Pileated Woodpeckers, Gray Catbirds, Carolina Wrens, Eastern Phoebes (winter), White-eyed Vireos, and a variety of woodland birds can be seen and heard along the trail. Winter paddlers may happen upon a family of River Otters and be treated to an exhibition of their energetic antics.

At Red Trail mile 26.1 you reach the southwestern entrance to Floyds Prairie. The Green Trail enters on the eastern side of the river, but this section of it is not open to day-use boating. By this point, the river has changed character again. Broad and sweeping, it passes through a mixed forest of Pond Cypress, bays, hollies, and Red Maple. The quiet backwaters attract Wood Ducks, Anhingas, and alligators.

The next 2 miles offer pleasant paddling along the gently curving river channel. You will hit another trail junction 7.7 miles from the boat ramp (Red Trail 24.1). A spur of the Red Trail leaves the river on the eastern side and leads to the Big Water overnight shelter and Floyds Prairie. As with the Green Trail, this trail is limited to permit holders and refuge staff.

Soon after the junction with the Red Trail Spur you enter the enchanted region of Big Water Lake. Here the river widens and becomes quite still. Large cypresses line the shores and reflect beautifully on the calm, dark waters. A day-use rest shelter is located along the eastern side of the lake about 1 mile past the junction with the Red Trail Spur. Though a nice spot to take a break, it is hard to forsake your boat while paddling the placid waters of the lake.

The trail is open to day-use boating to the top of the lake (Red Trail mile 21), though only the most determined and best-conditioned paddlers are likely to be able to complete the 21.6-mile round trip in a day.

26 Orange Trail

Distance: 2.2 miles.

See map on page 125

Difficulty: Easy.
Start: Stephen C. Foster State Park boat ramp.
End: Billys Island.
Type of trail: Canal, natural channel.
Hazards: Motorboats, lightning, airboats, alligators, biting insects.
Habitats: Wooded swamp, lake.
Reliability: Good.
USGS map: Billys Island-GA.
Visitor use: Moderate to heavy; open to public motorboat use.

Overview: From Stephen C. Foster State Park, you paddle east across Billys Lake to the boat dock on Billys Island. The short trip provides nice views of Billys Lake and gives you the option of exploring the environs and artifacts on Billys Island via the walking trail. Wildlife viewing can be rewarding. Watch for alligators, aquatic turtles, Anhingas, Pied-billed Grebes (winter), Ospreys, and Prothonotary Warblers (summer). The lake and the island are popular areas, so you can expect to encounter a variety of other visitors, including motorboat operators, tour boats, canoeists, kayakers, anglers, and sightseers. The deep water of the lake and canal close only during the most severe droughts.

The trail: From the Stephen C. Foster boat ramp (a fee is charged), paddle north up the 0.4-mile-long canal to Billys Lake. When you reach the lake, turn right and follow the lake along its arching course to the east. It doesn't take long to see why Billys Lake is so popular. The contrast of still, dark waters and overhanging cypresses are what most people envision when they think of the Okefenokee.

If you are setting a leisurely pace, it is worth nosing into the many nooks and backwaters that dot the shoreline. Billys Lake harbors a variety of wildlife, and by paddling quietly along its edges and keeping a watchful eye you are likely to see what many others miss: whirligig beetles, water striders, Emerald Jewelwings, Tiger Swallowtails, Florida Cricket Frogs, Florida Cooters, baby alligators (not too close), Brown Water Snakes, Green Anoles, and a multitude of dragonflies.

In a little more than 1 mile down the lake, the Middle Fork of the Suwannee River, and the path of the Red Trail, enters the lake from the north. East of this junction, Billys Lake narrows to about 50 yards wide. Much of the shore is lined by a low, dense growth of Black Gum and Pond Cypress. A few thickly vegetated backwaters jut off from the north shore and are good places to look for alligators, aquatic turtles, White Ibis, Snowy Egret, and Little Blue Heron. Don't be fooled by the white plumage of the immature Little Blues. Little Blue Herons don't attain the deep slate blue color of adults until their second year. Check the bill and leg color to be sure—immature Little Blue Herons have a dark-tipped, pale blue bill and dull greenish legs.

Billys Island lies 0.7 mile past the junction with the Middle Fork of the Suwannee. A wooden boat dock sits on the south shore of the lake and provides easy access to the island. Billys is the Okefenokee's third largest island (3,300 acres). It is one of the big sand islands formed by the sea long before the Okefenokee existed. A walking trail starts at the base of the dock and makes a short loop around the northern tip of the island (secure or carry your valuables). The trail gives you a chance to the see the Slash Pine, Saw Palmetto, Live Oak, and Sweetgum woods that grow on the island as well as the numerous artifacts of past human habitation.

Billys Island has a rich and colorful human history. At various times it was used as a refuge for remnant bands of Seminoles, a homestead for early Swampers, and the site of a booming lumber town complete with movie theater. Most evidence of all that is gone now. What's left are the skeletal remains—burial mounds, cemeteries, and the steel framework of cars and equipment. Walking amid the quiet regrowth of trees and bushes, it is almost surreal to envision a bustling town with sawmill, schoolhouse, and dance hall.

The Orange Trail is open to day-use boating for another 0.1 mile beyond Billys Island. Past that, the trail is open only to permit holders and refuge staff.

27 Brown Trail

Distance: 4.6 miles; plus additional trails.
See map on page 130
Difficulty: Moderate.
Start: Stephen C. Foster State Park boat ramp.
End: Suwannee River Sill.
Type of trail: Canal, natural channel.
Hazards: Motorboats, airboats, alligators, biting insects.
Habitats: Wooded swamp, lake.
Reliability: Moderate to good.
USGS maps: Billys Island-GA, The Pocket-GA.
Visitor use: Moderate to heavy; open to public motorboat use.

Overview: You can follow the first 4.6 miles of the Brown Trail from Stephen C. Foster State Park to the Suwannee River Sill. The trip takes you across the open landscape of Billys Lake and down the wooded path of the Suwannee River. A variety of wildlife can be seen, including alligators, aquatic turtles, Anhingas, White Ibis, Great Egrets, Red-bellied Woodpeckers, Carolina Wrens, and Prothonotary Warblers (summer). Most of the people entering the swamp at Stephen C. Foster State Park head east up the lake, so the western side of the lake via the Brown Trail is your best bet for getting away from the crowds. Still, the whole area is a popular

The privy is a rare sign of civilization in the Okefenokee wilderness.

destination, and you should expect to encounter motorboat operators and other paddlers along the way. The river portion of the trail is susceptible to drought and is occasionally closed due to low water.

The trail: Take the 0.4-mile-long canal north from the Stephen C. Foster State Park boat ramp (a fee is charged) to Billys Lake. At the lake, turn left (west) and head down the lake. Billys Lake is about 100 yards wide and, except for an irregular fringe of Spatterdock, is mostly free of vegetation. On quiet foggy mornings, the dark glassy waters and snaggled cypress along its borders make a stirring sight.

As you paddle down the lake keep an eye out for Ospreys, Anhingas, Wood Ducks, and Pied-billed Grebes (winter). The Spatterdock-covered backwaters often hold Great Egrets or Little Blue Herons. The cypress, gum, and bay woods around the lake are a good place to find Prothonotary and Yellow-throated Warblers in the spring. And don't forget to watch for the Okefenokee's most popular denizen, the American Alligator.

At mile 1.6 the lake forks. The right fork heads northwest for 0.4 mile, then ends in a wall of trees and thick shrubs. It is open to day-use paddling and worth exploring if you are in the mood for a short side trip. If you are desperate to see an alligator and haven't yet, definitely check the right fork. Alligators can often be found on this quiet stretch of the lake long after the stream of tourists has chased them into hiding in other areas.

To continue down the Brown Trail, follow the left fork to the southwest. Past the fork, the lake narrows considerably and is rimmed by a squat, scrubby forest of Black Gum and Pond Cypress. For some reason, this part of the lake always seems devoid of wildlife, and you will likely have an uneventful 0.2-mile paddle to the end of the lake.

At the western end of the lake, the water gathers into the 20-yard-wide channel of the Suwannee River and enters a shady forest of Black Gum, Pond Cypress, Red Maple, Dahoon Holly, and Swamp Bay. The crowns of opposing trees flow together overhead and form an irregular canopy above the sun-dappled trail. Titi, Hurrah Bush, Virginia Sweetspire, and Poor-man's Soap divvy up space along the banks and hang out over the watercourse.

If you are paddling at low water, be sure to watch for the line of old logging tram posts that cross the trail just as you leave the lake and hit the river. At high water they are safely submerged. At low water they lie just below the surface or stick out of the water creating a real hazard.

In a short time you pass the Mixons Hammock overnight stop. The area is reserved for special groups and is not open to day-use paddlers.

Past Mixons Hammock the river channel constricts as you enter the Narrows. For the next 0.7 mile the trail twists and turns as the Suwannee River slithers over the low rise at the base of Billys Lake. The 6- to 25-foot-wide channel seems to go in every direction save straight. Abrupt curves and ambits around trees alternate with meandering bends and sluggish pools. Submerged stumps and logs create unexpected obstacles. Though not technically challenging, you will probably be making good use of your draw, pry, and sweep strokes.

Currents through the Narrows are typically moderate (1 to 2 miles per hour) but vary depending on water levels. Just remember that whatever paddling boost you get on the way down will have to be overcome on the way back.

Around you, Gray Squirrels, Red-bellied Woodpeckers, Blue Jays, Common Grackles, Northern Flickers, Carolina Wrens, and White-eyed Vireos scuttle through the woods and liven up the trip with their exuberant calls and songs. Though the shady woods are not especially blessed with an abundance of wildflowers, mats of Hatpins and patches of Spatterdock brighten the way with their blossoms through-out much of the year. Not to be outdone, many of the shrubs along the river course have showy flowers, which bloom in early spring. One wildflower display that merits special mention is that of the Climbing Heath. Though not much to look at throughout most of the year, this meager vine produces a profusion of elegant, white flowers in February and March.

Passing out of the Narrows, the river widens to 15 to 30 feet and becomes gently curving. The forest canopy thins as Black Gum and Pond Cypress predominate. Backwaters of Spatterdock and yellow-eyed grasses and shrubby openings of Titi and Hurrah Bush become regular features along the trail.

By mile 2.8 the surrounding woods have stepped back, and the river is bordered by a wide band of Spatterdock. Sprinkled with old cypress stumps and a variety of shrubs, the sunny Spatterdock belt is a favorite foraging area for White Ibis, Little Blue Herons, and Great Egrets.

At mile 3.4, the forest reclaims its hold on the river as a mix of cypress and gum close in on the channel. Then in another 0.2 mile, the Pond Cypress and Black Gum yield to a low forest of Ogeechee Lime. Scattered cypresses grow amid the lime and often serve as perches for vultures and Anhingas. Alligators and aquatic turtles can be found swimming in the trail or across the watery expanses beneath the trees.

Paddling among the bent, twisted, shadowy shapes of the Ogeechee Lime, you are apt to believe every folk tale ever told of the Okefenokee—tales of sun maidens and ferocious warriors, lost islands of paradise, Mayan explorers, and prankster spirits called "haints" because they "h'ain't quite alive but h'ain't quite dead." All of which is part of the Okefenokee's appeal, an enduring air of mystery.

The trail continues its winding course through the Ogeechee Lime forest until reaching the Suwannee River Sill at mile 4.6. At the sill, the Brown Trail turns to the north and continues up the sill channel on its way to Cravens Hammock. The entire sill channel is open to day-use boating (see Suwannee River Sill Day-Use Trails, page 109).

A Final Note

This guide is an attempt to provide canoeists and kayakers with information about typical conditions encountered while paddling in the Okefenokee National Wildlife Refuge. Be aware that your particular experience may be significantly different. The Okefenokee, while it has been here for more than 5,000 years, is constantly rearranging itself. Water levels, weather, vegetation, wildlife, facilities, and regulations vary from season to season and year to year. In some years they vary more than others. We have seen the Suwannee River nearly breaching the sill, and we have seen it barely trickling through the sill gates. We have seen Chesser Prairie as a watery expanse and as a drying bed of peat exposed to the sun. Please use this guide along with your common sense and the latest information on regulations, weather, and water levels. Be safe and have fun.

Trail Maps

The trail maps in the following pages were developed from a classified satellite image of the Okefenokee National Wildlife Refuge and digital versions of the 1994 series of United States Geological Survey (USGS) 1:24,000 quadrangle maps. Magnetic declination on the trail maps is between 3.5 and 4 degrees west.

MAP LEGEND

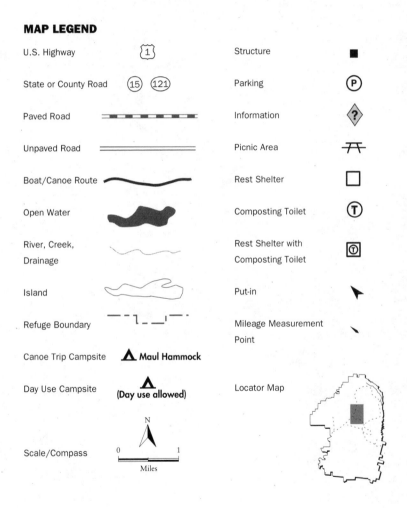

U.S. Highway	(1)	Structure	■
State or County Road	(15) (121)	Parking	(P)
Paved Road		Information	?
Unpaved Road		Picnic Area	🪑
Boat/Canoe Route		Rest Shelter	□
Open Water		Composting Toilet	(T)
River, Creek, Drainage		Rest Shelter with Composting Toilet	
Island		Put-in	
Refuge Boundary		Mileage Measurement Point	
Canoe Trip Campsite	▲ Maul Hammock		
Day Use Campsite	▲ (Day use allowed)	Locator Map	
Scale/Compass	N 0 —— 1 Miles		

See map on page 123.

See map on page 126.

Big Water Lake

Red Trail

Dinner Point

Saw Prairie

Prairie

Maui Hammock

Maui Hammock Lake

Red Trail

7.3

Couthouse Island

Christmas Lake

Obu Lake

Pond Lake

Picnic Lake

Boat Landing Island

Gum Slough

Double Lakes

6.2

Carters Prairie

2.7

Green

0.8

0.4

Red Trail

0.5 Trout Lake

0.6

Elder North Lake

0.2

0.4 Kingfisher Landing

T P

Kingfisher Landing Road

1

Prairie

Shrubland

Wooded Swamp

N

0   1

Miles

122

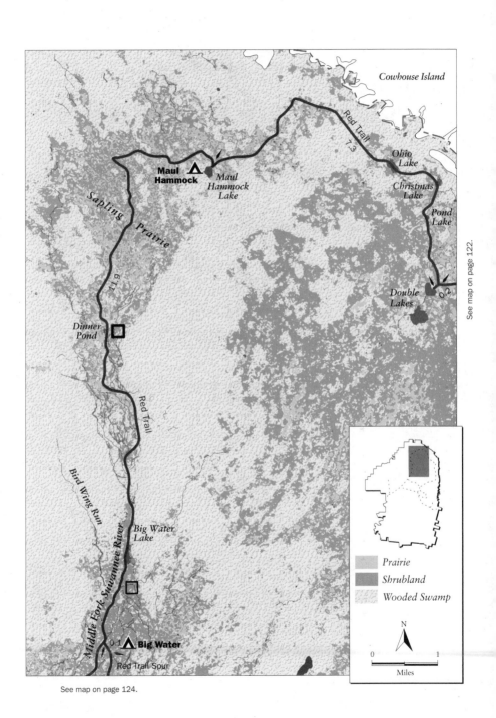

Cowhouse Island

Red Trail

7.3

Ohio Lake

Christmas Lake

Pond Lake

Maul Hammock

Maul Hammock Lake

Sapling Prairie

11.9

Double Lakes

0.2

See map on page 122.

Dinner Pond

Red Trail

Bird Wing Run

Big Water Lake

Middle Fork Suwannee River

0.1 Big Water

Red Trail Spur

See map on page 124.

Prairie

Shrubland

Wooded Swamp

N

0   1

Miles

See map on page 123.

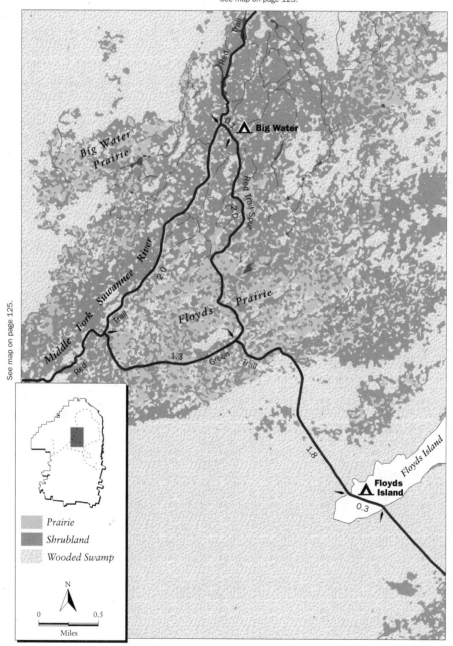

See map on page 125.

See map on page 125.

See map on page 130.

Brown Trail

0.4

Billys

1.2

0.4

The Pocket

17

Jones Island

Developed Campground

P

?

Stephen C. Foster State Park

Billys Lake

1.1

Boat dock

Billys Island

Prairie
Shrubland
Wooded Swamp

0
Miles
1

N

Minnies Island

Camp Island

Red Trail

4.2

Minnies Lake

Middle Fork Suwannee River

Red Trail

2.0

Floyds

1.3

Green Trail

2.0

Big Water Prairie

Red Trail Spur

0.1

Big Water

East Fork Suwannee River

6.1

Orange Trail

Canal Run
(Day use allowed)

0.2

1.8

1.8

Blue Trail

0.8

Green Trail

1.0

0.3

Floyds Island

Floyds Island

Prairie

Purple Trail

Chase Prairie

See map on page 123.

See map on page 128.

See map on page 126.

See map on page 122.

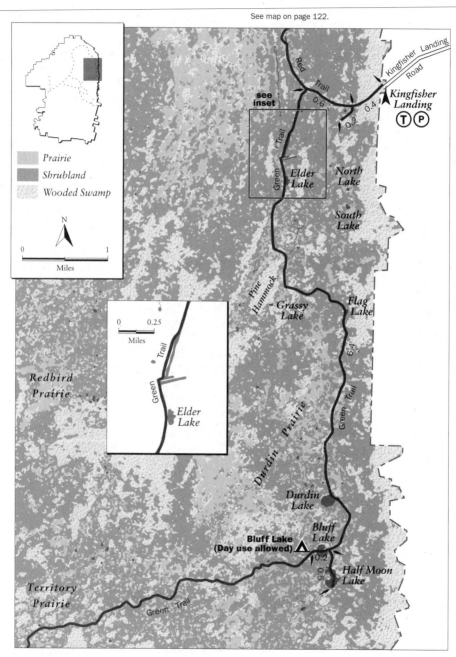

Prairie

Shrubland

Wooded Swamp

N

0   1

Miles

Kingfisher Landing Road

Kingfisher
Landing

(T) (P)

Red Trail

0.6

see
inset

Green Trail

Elder
Lake

North
Lake

0.2

0.4

South
Lake

Pine Hammock

Grassy
Lake

Flag
Lake

6.4

Green Trail

0   0.25

Miles

Green Trail

Elder
Lake

Redbird
Prairie

Durdin Prairie

Durdin
Lake

Bluff
Lake

Bluff Lake
(Day use allowed) △

0.2

0.5

Half Moon
Lake

Territory
Prairie

Green Trail

See map on page 127.

126

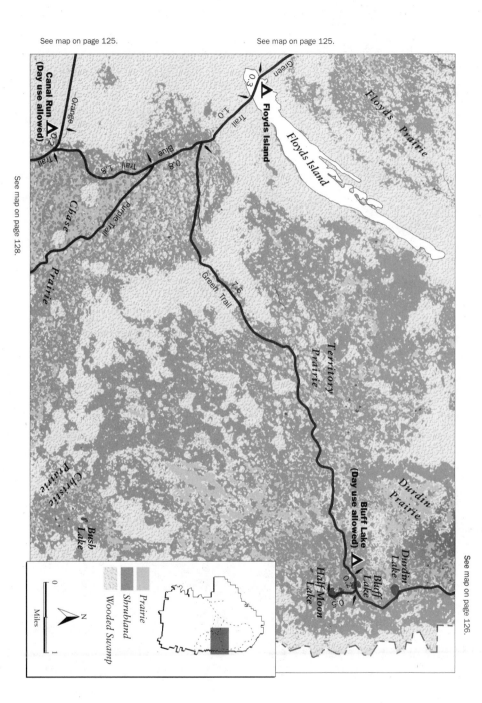

See map on page 125.

See map on page 125.

See map on page 128.

See map on page 126.

Canal Run
(Day use allowed)

Floyds Island

Floyds Prairie

Floyds Island

Orange

Trail

0.3

Green

1.0

Blue

Trail

0.8

1.8

Purple Trail

Chase

Prairie

Green Trail

7.6

Territory
Prairie

Christie

Prairie

Brush
Lake

Durdin
Prairie

Durdin
Lake

Bluff Lake
(Day use allowed)

Bluff
Lake

0.2

Half
Moon
Lake

0.5

Prairie
Shrubland
Wooded Swamp

N

0

1

Miles

See map on page 124.

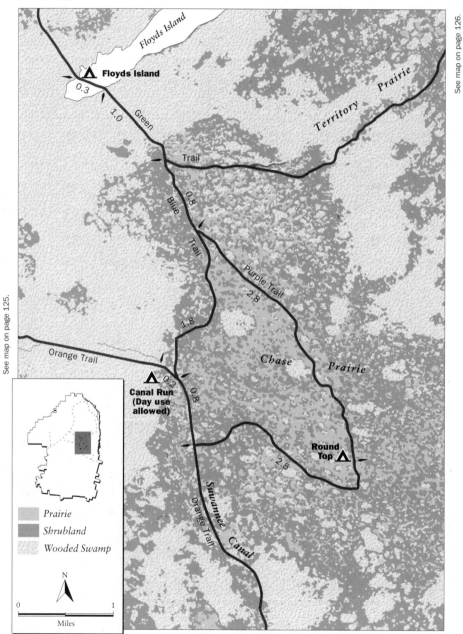

Floyds Island

0.3

1.0

Green

Trail

Blue

Trail

0.8

Purple Trail

2.8

1.8

Orange Trail

0.2

Canal Run
(Day use
allowed)

0.8

Chase   Prairie

Territory   Prairie

Round
Top

2.5

Suwannee   Canal

Orange Trail

Prairie

Shrubland

Wooded Swamp

N

0   1

Miles

See map on page 125.

See map on page 126.

See map on page 129.

See map on page 125.

See map on page 128.

See map on page 131.

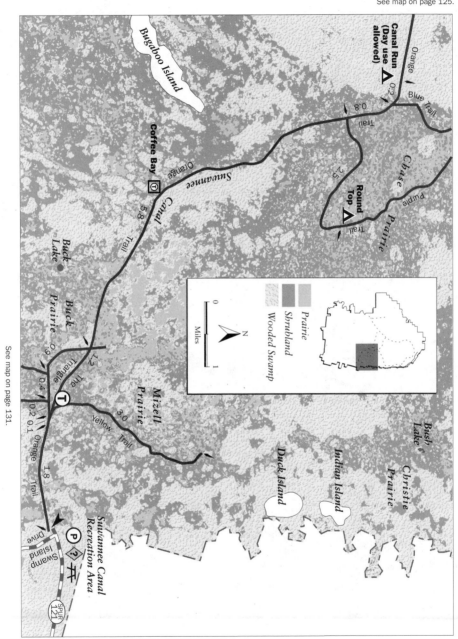

Bugaboo Island

Canal Run
(Day use
allowed) △

Orange

Blue Trail

Trail 0.8

0.2

Chase Prairie

2.5

Round
Top △

Purple Trail

Coffee Bay ⊤

Orange

Suwannee Canal

Trail 5.8

Buck
Lake

Buck
Prairie

0.9

The Triangle 1.2

0.4

⊤

0.2 0.1

Orange Trail

1.8

Yellow Trail

Mizell
Prairie 3.0

Bush
Lake

Christie Prairie

Indian Island

Duck Island

Suwannee Canal
Recreation Area

P ?

SPUR
121

Swamp Island Drive

N

Miles

0

1

Wooded Swamp
Shrubland
Prairie

129

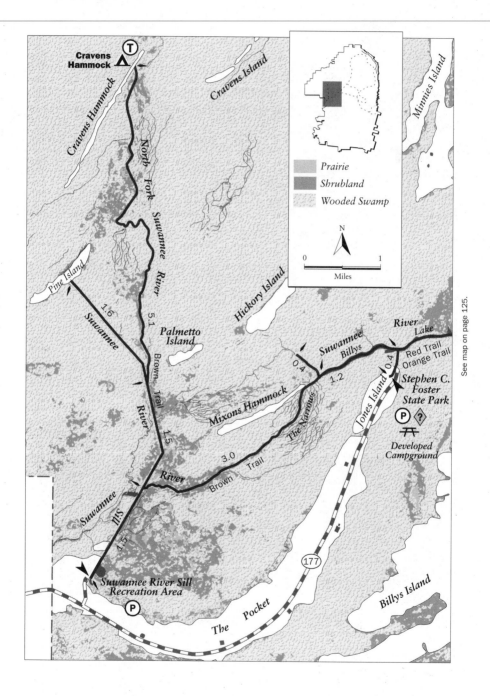

See map on page 125.

See map on page 129.

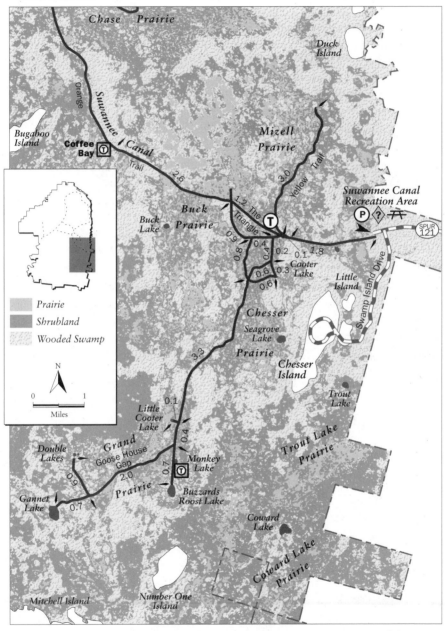

Selected Bibliography

Bartram, William. *The Travels of William Bartram*. Edited by Mark van Doren. New York: Dover, 1928.

Bent, A. C. *Life Histories of North American Birds of Prey. Part 1*. Smithsonian Institution United States National Museum Bulletin 167. Washington D.C.: United States Government Printing Office, 1937.

Cohen, A. D., D. J. Casagrande, M. J. Andrejko, and G. R. Best, editors. *The Okefenokee Swamp*. Los Alamos, N.M.: Wetland Surveys, 1984.

Forgey, William. *Wilderness Medicine*. Merrillville, Ind.: ICS Books, 1994.

Harmon, Will. *Leave No Trace*. Helena, Mont.: Falcon, 1997.

Harmon, Will. *Wild Country Companion*. Helena, Mont.: Falcon, 1994.

Isaac, Jeff and Peter Goff. *The Outward Bound Wilderness First-Aid Handbook*. New York: Lyons Press, 1991.

Laerm, Joshua and B. J. Freeman. *Fishes of the Okefenokee Swamp*. Athens, Ga.: University of Georgia Press, 1986.

Loftin, Cynthia. *Assessing patterns and processes of landscape change in Okefenokee Swamp, Ga*. Ph.D. Dissertation. Gainesville, Fla.: University of Florida, 1998.

Mason, Bill. *Song of the Paddle*. Toronto: Northword Press, 1988.

Matschat, Cecile. *Suwannee River*. New York: Rinehart and Company, 1938.

McQueen, A. S. and Hamp Mizell. *History of Okefenokee Swamp*. Clinton, S.C.: Jacobs and Company. 1926.

Russel, Franklin. *The Okefenokee Swamp*. New York: Time-Life Books, 1973.

Swedo, Suzanne. *Wilderness Survival*. Helena, Mont.: Falcon, 1998.

Appendix A

AUTHORS' RECOMMENDATIONS

Day-paddle for timid first-timers
19 Orange Trail from Suwannee Canal Recreation Area, page 98
24 Day-use trail along Suwannee River Sill, page 109
26 Orange Trail from Stephen C. Foster State Park, page 115

Day-paddle for parents with active children
24 Day-use trail along Suwannee River Sill, page 109
26 Orange Trail from Stephen C. Foster State Park, page 115

Day-paddle for adventurous intermediate or experienced paddlers
21 Day-use trails in Chesser and Grand prairies, page 103
25 Red Trail from Stephen C. Foster State Park, page 112
27 Brown Trail from Stephen C. Foster State Park, page 116

Day-paddle for nature lovers
21 Day-use trails in Chesser and Grand prairies, page 103
23 Green Trail from Kingfisher Landing, page 108
25 Red Trail from Stephen C. Foster State Park, page 112

Day-paddle for intermediate or experienced wilderness zealots
20 Yellow Trail, page 101
22 Red Trail from Kingfisher Landing, page 106
23 Green Trail from Kingfisher Landing, page 108

Overnighter for timid first-timers
Suwannee Canal Recreation Area–Canal Run–Suwannee Canal Recreation Area–
see Designated Overnight Trip 2; see chart on page 37.

Overnighter for adventurous first-timers
Kingfisher Landing–Bluff Lake–Kingfisher Landing–
see Designated Overnight Trip 1; see chart on page 37.

Overnighter for adventurous experienced paddlers
Suwannee Canal Recreation Area–Canal Run–Stephen C. Foster State Park–
see Designated Overnight Trip 2; see chart on page 37.
Stephen C. Foster State Park–Cravens Hammock–Stephen C. Foster State Park–
see Designated Overnight Trip 3; see chart on page 37.

Three-day getaway for intermediate or experienced paddlers
Kingfisher Landing–Bluff Lake–Round Top–Suwannee Canal Recreation Area–
see Designated Overnight Trip 6; see chart on page 37.

Kingfisher Landing–Bluff Lake–Floyds Island–Stephen C. Foster State Park–
see Designated Overnight Trip 5; see chart on page 37.

Suwannee Canal Recreation Area—Round Top—Floyds Island—Suwannee Canal
Recreation Area—see Designated Overnight Trip 7; see chart on pages 37 and 38.

Three-day getaway for experienced paddlers

Kingfisher Landing—Maul Hammock—Big Water—Stephen C. Foster State Park—
see Designated Overnight Trip 4; see chart on page 37.

Four-day tour for intermediate or experienced paddlers

Kingfisher Landing—Bluff Lake—Floyds Island—Canal Run—Stephen C. Foster
State Park—see Designated Overnight Trip 9; see chart on page 38.

Kingfisher Landing—Bluff Lake—Floyds Island—Round Top—Suwannee Canal
Recreation Area—see Designated Overnight Trip 10; see chart on page 38.

Five-day grand tour for experienced wilderness zealots

Kingfisher Landing—Maul Hammock—Big Water—Floyds Island—Bluff Lake—
Kingfisher Landing—see Designated Overnight Trip 11; see chart on page 38.

Kingfisher Landing—Maul Hammock—Big Water—Floyds Island—Canal Run—
Stephen C. Foster State Park—see Designated Overnight Trip 12; see chart on
page 38.

Appendix B

COMMON PLANTS OF THE OKEFENOKEE NATIONAL WILDLIFE REFUGE

Mosses

Family Sphagnidae
Sphagnum moss *(Sphagnum spp.)*

Ferns

Family Blechnaceae
Chain Fern *(Woodwardia virginica)*

Family Osmundaceae
Royal Fern *(Osmunda regalis)*

Family Polypodiaceae
Resurrection Fern *(Polypodium polypodioides)*

Conifers

Family Pinaceae
Slash Pine *(Pinus elliottii)*
Longleaf Pine *(Pinus palustris)*

Family Taxodiaceae
Pond Cypress *(Taxodium ascendens)*

Flowering Plants

Family Alismataceae
Arrowhead *(Sagittaria graminea)*

Family Gramineae
Plume Grass *(Erianthus brevibarbis)*
Broomsedge *(Andropogon virginicus)*
Maidencane *(Panicum hemitomon)*

Family Cyperaceae
Spikerush *(Eleocharis spp.)*
Three-way Sedge *(Dulichium arundinaceum)*
Beakrush *(Rhynchospora spp.)*
Walter's Sedge *(Carex walteriana)*

Family Arecaceae
Saw Palmetto *(Serenoa repens)*

Family Araceae
Neverwet *(Orontium aquaticum)*
Arrow Arum *(Peltandra sagittifolia)*

Family Xyridaceae
Yellow-eyed grass *(Xyris spp.)*

Family Eriocaulaceae
Hatpins *(Eriocaulon compressum)*

Family Bromeliaceae
Spanish Moss *(Tillandsia usneoides)*

Family Smilacaceae
Black Bamboo Vine *(Smilax laurifolia)*
Red Bamboo Vine *(Smilax walteri)*

Family Haemodoraceae
Redroot *(Lachnanthes caroliniana)*

Family Iridaceae
Southern Blue Flag *(Iris virginica)*

Family Orchidaceae
Grass Pink *(Calopogon tuberosus)*

Family Myricaceae
Wax Myrtle *(Myrica cerifera)*

Family Fagaceae
Live Oak *(Quercus virginiana)*
Water Oak *(Quercus nigra)*

Family Cabombaceae
Watershield *(Brasenia schreberi)*

Family Nymphaeaceae
Fragrant Water Lily *(Nymphaea odorata)*
Spatterdock *(Nuphar luteum)*

Family Magnoliaceae
Southern Magnolia *(Magnolia grandiflora)*
Sweetbay Magnolia *(Magnolia virginiana)*

Family Annonacae
Pawpaw *(Asimina spp.)*

Family Lauraceae
Red Bay *(Persea borbonia)*
Swamp Bay *(Persea palustris)*

Family Sarraceniaceae
Trumpet Leaf Pitcher Plant *(Sarracenia flava)*
Hooded Pitcher Plant *(Sarracenia minor)*
Parrot Pitcher Plant *(Sarracenia psittacina)*

Family Droseraceae
Narrow-leaved Sundew *(Drosera intermedia)*

Family Saxifragaceae
Virginia Sweetspire *(Itea virginica)*

Family Hamamelidaceae
Sweetgum *(Liquidambar styraciflua)*

Family Rosaceae
Sand Blackberry *(Rubus cuneifolius)*

Family Cyrillaceae
Black Titi *(Cliftonia monophylla)*
Titi *(Cyrilla racemiflora)*

Family Aquifoliaceae
Dahoon Holly *(Ilex cassine)*
Gallberry *(Ilex glabra)*
Large Gallberry *(Ilex coriacea)*

Family Aceraceae
Red Maple *(Acer rubrum)*

Family Vitaceae
Muscadine *(Vitis rotundifolia)*

Family **Theaceae**
Loblolly Bay *(Gordonia lasianthus)*

Family **Lythraceae**
Swamp Loosestrife *(Decodon verticillatus)*

Family **Nyssaceae**
Ogeechee Lime *(Nyssa ogeche)*
Black Gum *(Nyssa sylvatica)*

Family **Melastomataceae**
Meadow Beauty *(Rhexia mariana)*

Family **Clethraceae**
Poor-man's Soap *(Clethra alnifolia)*

Family **Ericaceae**
Swamp Fetterbush *(Leucothoe racemosa)*
Hurrah Bush *(Lyonia lucida)*
Climbing Heath *(Pieris phillyreifolia)*

Family **Lentibulariaceae**
Bladderwort *(Utricularia* spp.*)*

Family **Rubiaceae**
Buttonbush *(Cephalanthus occidentalis)*

Family **Compositae**
Beggar Ticks *(Bidens mitis)*

Appendix C

VERTEBRATES OF THE OKEFENOKEE NATIONAL WILDLIFE REFUGE

Fish

Family Lepisosteidae
Florida Gar *(Lepisosteus platyrhincus)*

Family Amiidae
Bowfin *(Amia calva)*

Family Anguillidae
American Eel *(Anguilla rostrata)*

Family Esocidae
Redfin Pickerel *(Esox americanus americanus)*
Chain Pickerel *(Esox niger)*

Family Umbridae
Eastern Mudminnow *(Umbra pygmaea)*

Family Catostomidae
Lake Chubsucker *(Erimyzon sucetta)*
Spotted Chubsucker *(Minytrema melanops)*

Family Ictaluridae
Yellow Bullhead *(Ictalurus natalis)*
Brown Bullhead *(Ictalurus nebulosus)*
Channel Catfish *(Ictalurus punctatus)*
Tadpole Madtom *(Noturus gyrinus)*
Speckled Madtom *(Noturus leptacanthus)*

Family Aphredoderidae
Pirate Perch *(Aphredoderus sayanus)*

Family Cyprinodontidae
Golden Topminnow *(Fundulus chrysotus)*
Banded Topminnow *(Fundulus cingulatus)*
Lined Topminnow *(Fundulus lineolatus)*
Starhead Topminnow *(Fundulus notti)*
Pygmy Killifish *(Leptolucania ommata)*

Family Poeciliidae
Mosquitofish *(Gambusia affinis)*
Least Killifish *(Heterandria formosa)*

Family Atherinidae
Brook Silverside *(Labidesthes sicculus)*

Family Elassomidae
Everglades Pygmy Sunfish *(Elassoma evergladei)*
Okefenokee Pygmy Sunfish *(Elassoma okefenokee)*

Family Centrarchidae
Mud Sunfish *(Acantharchus pomotis)*
Flier *(Centrarchus macropterus)*
Blackbanded Sunfish *(Enneacanthus chaetodon)*
Bluespotted Sunfish *(Enneacanthus gloriosus)*
Banded Sunfish *(Enneacanthus obesus)*
Redbreast Sunfish *(Lepomis auritus)*

Warmouth *(Lepomis gulosus)*
Bluegill *(Lepomis macrochirus)*
Dollar Sunfish *(Lepomis marginatus)*
Spotted Sunfish *(Lepomis punctatus)*
Largemouth Bass *(Micropterus salmoides)*
Black Crappie *(Pomoxis nigromaculatus)*

Family Percidae
Scalyhead Darter *(Etheostoma barratti)*
Swamp Darter *(Etheostoma fusiforme)*
Blackbanded Darter *(Percina nigrofasciata)*

Toads and Frogs

Family Bufonidae
Oak Toad *(Bufo quercicus)*
Southern Toad *(Bufo terrestris)*

Family Hylidae
Florida Cricket Frog *(Acris gryllus dorsalis)*
Gray Treefrog *(Hyla chrysoscelis)*
Green Treefrog *(Hyla cinerea cinerea)*
Southern Spring Peeper *(Hyla crucifer bartramiana)*
Pinewoods Treefrog *(Hyla femoralis)*
Barking Treefrog *(Hyla gratiosa)*
Squirrel Treefrog *(Hyla squirella)*
Little Grass Frog *(Pseudacris ocularis)*
Southern Chorus Frog *(Pseudacris nigrita nigrita)*
Ornate Chorus Frog *(Pseudacris ornata)*

Family Microhylidae
Eastern Narrowmouth Toad *(Gastrophryne carolinensis)*

Family Pelobatidae
Eastern Spadefoot Toad *(Scaphiopus holbrooki holbrooki)*

Family Ranidae
Florida Gopher Frog *(Rana areolata aescpus)*
Bullfrog *(Rana catesbeiana)*
Bronze Frog *(Rana clamitans clamitans)*
Pig Frog *(Rana grylio)*
River Frog *(Rana heckscheri)*
Southern Leopard Frog *(Rana utricularia)*
Carpenter Frog *(Rana virgatipes)*

Salamanders

Family Ambystomatidae
Flatwoods Salamander *(Ambystoma cingulatum)*
Marbled Salamander *(Ambystoma opacum)*
Mole Salamander *(Ambystoma talpoideum)*
Tiger Salamander *(Ambystoma tigrinum)*

Family Amphiumidae
Two-toed Amphiuma *(Amphiuma means)*

Family Plethodontidae
Southern Dusky Salamander *(Desmognathus auriculatus)*
Southern Two-lined Salamander *(Eurycea cirriger)*
Dwarf Salamander *(Eurycea quadridigitata)*
Slimy Salamander *(Plethodon glutinosus glutinosus)*
Mud Salamander *(Pseudotriton montanus)*
Many-lined Salamander *(Stereochilus marginatus)*

Family Salamandridae
Red-spotted Newt *(Notophthalmus viridescens)*
Striped Newt *(Notophthalmus perstriatus)*

Family Sirenidae
Dwarf Siren *(Pseudobranchus striatus)*
Eastern Lesser Siren *(Siren intermedia intermedia)*
Greater Siren *(Siren lacertina)*

Alligators and Crocodiles

Family Alligatoridae
American Alligator *(Alligator mississippiensis)*

Turtles

Family Chelydridae
Common Snapping Turtle *(Chelydra serpentina serpentina)*
Alligator Snapping Turtle *(Macroclemys temmincki)*

Family Emydidae
Eastern Chicken Turtle *(Deirochelys reticularia reticularia)*
Florida Cooter *(Pseudemys floridana floridana)*
Florida Redbelly Turtle *(Pseudemys nelsoni)*
Florida Box Turtle *(Terrapene carolina bauri)*
Eastern Box Turtle *(Terrapene carolina carolina)*
Yellowbelly Turtle *(Trachemys scripta scripta)*
Red-eared Slider *(Trachemys scripta elegans)*

Family Kinosternidae
Striped Mud Turtle *(Kinosternon bauri palmarum)*
Eastern Mud Turtle *(Kinosternon subrubum subrubum)*
Loggerhead Musk Turtle *(Sternotherus minor minor)*
Stinkpot *(Sternotherus odoratus)*

Family Testudinidae
Gopher Tortoise *(Gopherus polyphemus)*

Family Trionychidae
Florida Softshell *(Trionyx ferox)*

Lizards

Family Anguidae
Eastern Slender Glass Lizard *(Ophisaurus attenuatus longicaudus)*
Island Glass Lizard *(Ophisaurus compressus)*
Eastern Glass Lizard *(Ophisaurus ventralis)*

Family Iguanidae
Green Anole *(Anolis carolinensis)*
Southern Fence Lizard *(Sceloporus undulatus undulatus)*

Family Scincidae
Northern Mole Skink *(Eumeces egregius similis)*
Five-lined Skink *(Eumeces fasciatus)*
Southeastern Five-lined Skink *(Eumeces inexpectatus)*
Broadheaded Skink *(Eumeces laticeps)*
Ground Skink *(Scincella lateralis)*

Family Teiidae
Six-lined Racerunner *(Cnemidophorus sexlineatus sexlineatus)*

Snakes

Family Colubridae
Northern Scarlet Snake *(Cemophora coccinea copei)*
Southern Black Racer *(Coluber constrictor priapus)*
Southern Ringneck Snake *(Diadophis punctatus punctatus)*
Eastern Indigo Snake *(Drymarchon corais couperi)*
Corn Snake *(Elaphe guttata guttata)*
Yellow Rat Snake *(Elaphe obsoleta quadrivittata)*
Gray Rat Snake *(Elaphe obsoleta spiloides)*
Eastern Mud Snake *(Farancia abacura abacura)*
Rainbow Snake *(Farancia erytrogramma)*
Eastern Hognose Snake *(Heterodon platyrhinos)*
Southern Hognose Snake *(Heterodon simus)*
Mole Kingsnake *(Lampropeltis calligaster rhombomaculata)*
Eastern Kingsnake *(Lampropeltis getulus)*
Scarlet Kingsnake *(Lampropeltis triangulum elapsoides)*
Eastern Coachwhip *(Masticophis flagellum flagellum)*
Florida Green Water Snake *(Nerodia cyclopion floridana)*
Plainbelly Water Snake *(Nerodia erythrogaster)*
Banded Water Snake *(Nerodia fasciata fasciata)*
Florida Banded Water Snake *(Nerodia fasciata pictiventris)*

Brown Water Snake *(Nerodia taxispilota)*
Rough Green Snake *(Opheodrys aestivus)*
Florida Pine Snake *(Pituophis melanoleucus mugitis)*
Striped Crayfish Snake *(Regina alleni)*
Glossy Crayfish Snake *(Regina rigida rigida)*
Pine Woods Snake *(Rhadinaea flavilata)*
North Forida Swamp Snake *(Seminatrix pygaea pygaea)*
Florida Brown Snake *(Storeria dekayi victa)*
Florida Redbelly Snake *(Storeria occipitomaculata obscura)*
Ribbon Snake *(Thamnophis sauritus)*
Eastern Garter Snake *(Thamnophis sirtalis sirtalis)*
Rough Earth Snake *(Virginia striatula)*
Smooth Earth Snake *(Virginia valeriae valeriae)*

Family Elapidae
Eastern Coral Snake *(Micrurus fulvius)*

Family Viperidae
Florida Cottonmouth *(Agkistrodon piscivorus conanti)*
Eastern Diamondback Rattlesnake *(Crotalus adamanteus)*
Canebrake Rattlesnake *(Crotalus horridus atricaudatus)*
Dusky Pygmy Rattlesnake *(Sistrurus milarius barbouri)*

Mammals
Family Didelphidae
Virginia Opossum *(Didelphis virginiana pigna)*

Family Soricidae
Southern Short-tailed Shrew *(Blarina carolinensis)*
Least Shrew *(Cryptotus parva parva)*

Family Talpidae
Eastern Mole *(Scalopus aquaticus australis)*
Star-nosed Mole *(Condylura cristata)*

Family Vespertillionidae
Southeastern Myotis *(Myotis austroriparius austroriparius)*
Eastern Pipistrelle *(Pipistrellus subflavus subflavus)*
Rafinesque's Big-eared Bat *(Plecotus rafinesquii)*
Big Brown Bat *(Eptesicus fuscus fuscus)*
Hoary Bat *(Lasiurus cinereus cinereus)*
Red Bat *(Lasiurus borealis borealis)*
Seminole Bat *(Lasiurus seminolus)*
Yellow Bat *(Lasiurus intermedius floridanus)*
Evening Bat *(Nycticeius humeralis)*

Family Molossidae
Brazilian Free-tailed Bat *(Tadarida brasiliensis)*

Family Dasypodidae
Nine-banded Armadillo *(Dasypus novemcinctus mexicanus)*

Family Leporidae
Eastern Cottontail *(Sylvilagus floridanus mallurus)*
Marsh Rabbit *(Sylvilagus palustris palustris)*

Family Sciuridae
Gray Squirrel *(Sciurus carolinensis carolinensis)*
Fox Squirrel *(Sciurus niger niger)*
Southern Flying Squirrel *(Glaucomys volans querceti)*

Family Geomyidae
Georgia Pocket Gopher *(Geomys pinetis pinetis)*
Southeastern Pocket Gopher *(Geomys pinetis floridanus)*

Family Castoridae
Beaver *(Castor canadensis carolinensis)*

Family Cricetidae
Eastern Woodrat *(Neotoma floridana floridana)*
Hispid Cotton Rat *(Sigmodon hispidus hispidus)*
Eastern Harvest Mouse *(Reithrodontomys humilus humilus)*
Marsh Rice Rat *(Oryzomys palustris palustris)*
Oldfield Mouse *(Peromyscus poliontous polionotus)*
Cotton Mouse *(Peromyscus gossypinus)*
Golden Mouse *(Ochrotomys nuttalli aureolis)*
Pine Vole *(Microtus pinetorum)*
Round-tailed Muskrat *(Neofiber alleni exoristus)*

Family Muridae
House Mouse *(Mus musculus musculus)*
Black Rat *(Rattus rattus rattus)*
Roof Rat *(Rattus rattus alexandrinus)*
Norway Rat *(Rattus norvegicus)*

Family Ursidae
Black Bear *(Ursus americanus floridanus)*

Family Procyonidae
Raccoon *(Procyon lotor elucus)*

Family Mustelidae
Mink *(Mustela vison)*
Long-tailed Weasel *(Mustela frenata olivacea)*
Striped Skunk *(Mephitis mephitis elongata)*
River Otter *(Lutra canadensis vaga)*

Family Canidae
Gray Fox *(Urocyon cinereoargenteus floridanus)*
Red Fox *(Vulpes vulpes)*

Family Felidae
Bobcat *(Felis rufus)*

Family Suidae
Wild Pig *(Sus scrofa)*

Family Cerivade
White-tailed Deer *(Odocoileus virginianus)*

Birds

Family Gaviidae
Common Loon *(Gavia immer)*

Family Podicipedidae
Pied-billed Grebe *(Podilymbus podiceps)*
Horned Grebe *(Podiceps auritus)*

Family Pelecanidae
American White Pelican *(Pelecanus erythrorhynchos)*
Brown Pelican *(Pelecanus occidentalis)*

Family Phalacrocoracidae
Double-crested Cormorant *(Phalacrocorax auritus)*

Family Anhingidae
Anhinga *(Anhinga anhinga)*

Ardeidae
American Bittern *(Botaurus lentiginosus)*
Least Bittern *(Ixobrychus exilis)*
Great Blue Heron *(Ardea herodias)*
Great Egret *(Casmerodius albus)*
Snowy Egret *(Egretta thula)*
Little Blue Heron *(Egretta caerulea)*
Tricolored Heron *(Egretta tricolor)*
Cattle Egret *(Bubulcus ibis)*
Green Heron *(Butorides virescens)*
Black-crowned Night-Heron *(Nycticorax nycticorax)*
Yellow-crowned Night-Heron *(Nyctanassa violacea)*

Family Threskiornithidae
White Ibis *(Eudocimus albus)*
Glossy Ibis *(Plegadis falcinellus)*
Roseate Spoonbill *(Ajaia ajaja)*

Family Ciconiidae
Wood Stork *(Mycteria americana)*

Family Anatidae
Tundra Swan *(Cygnus columbianus)*
Snow Goose *(Chen caerulescens)*
Canada Goose *(Branta canadensis)*
Wood Duck *(Aix sponsa)*
Green-winged Teal *(Anas crecca)*
American Black Duck *(Anas rubripes)*
Mallard *(Anas platyrhynchos)*
Northern Pintail *(Anas acuta)*
Blue-winged Teal *(Anas discors)*
Northern Shoveler *(Anas clypeata)*
Gadwall *(Anas strepera)*
Eurasian Wigeon *(Anas penelope)*

American Wigeon *(Anas americana)*
Canvasback *(Aythya valisineria)*
Redhead *(Aythya americana)*
Ring-necked Duck *(Aythya collaris)*
Greater Scaup *(Aythya marila)*
Lesser Scaup *(Aytha affinis)*
Common Goldeneye *(Bucephala clangula)*
Bufflehead *(Bucephala albeola)*
Hooded Merganser *(Lophodytes cucullatus)*
Common Merganser *(Mergus merganser)*
Red-breasted Merganser *(Mergus serrator)*
Ruddy Duck *(Oxyura jamaicensis)*

Family Cathartidae
Black Vulture *(Coragyps atratus)*
Turkey Vulture *(Cathartes aura)*

Family Accipitridae
Osprey *(Pandion haliaetus)*
Swallow-tailed Kite *(Elanoides forficatus)*
Mississippi Kite *(Ictinia mississippiensis)*
Bald Eagle *(Haliaeetus leucocephalus)*
Northern Harrier *(Circus cyaneus)*
Sharp-shinned Hawk *(Accipiter striatus)*
Cooper's Hawk *(Accipiter cooperii)*
Red-shouldered Hawk *(Buteo lineatus)*
Broad-winged Hawk *(Buteo platypterus)*
Red-tailed Hawk *(Buteo jamaicensis)*
Rough-legged Hawk *(Buteo lagopus)*
Golden Eagle *(Aquila chrysaetos)*

Family Falconidae
American Kestrel *(Falco sparverius)*
Merlin *(Falco columbarius)*
Peregrine Falcon *(Falco peregrinus)*

Family Phasianidae
Wild Turkey *(Meleagris gallopavo)*
Northern Bobwhite *(Colinus virginianus)*

Family Rallidae
Yellow Rail *(Coturnicops noveboracensis)*
Clapper Rail *(Rallus longirostris)*
King Rail *(Rallus elegans)*
Virginia Rail *(Rallus limicola)*
Sora *(Porzana carolina)*
Purple Gallinule *(Porphyrula martinica)*
Common Moorhen *(Gallinula chloropus)*
American Coot *(Fulica americana)*

Family Aramidae
Limpkin *(Aramus guarauna)*

Family Gruidae
Sandhill Crane *(Grus canadensis)*

Family Charadriidae
Semipalmated Plover *(Charadrius semipalmatus)*
Killdeer *(Charadrius vociferus)*

Family Scolopacidae
Greater Yellowlegs *(Tringa melanoleuca)*
Lesser Yellowlegs *(Tringa flavipes)*

Solitary Sandpiper *(Tringa solitaria)*
Willet *(Catoptrophorus semipalmatus)*
Spotted Sandpiper *(Actitis macularia)*
Whimbrel *(Numenius phaeopus)*
Sanderling *(Calidris alba)*
Semipalmated Sandpiper *(Calidris pusilla)*
Western Sandpiper *(Calidris mauri)*
Dunlin *(Calidris alpina)*
Short-billed Dowitcher *(Limnodromus griseus)*
Common Snipe *(Gallinago gallinago)*
American Woodcock *(Scolopax minor)*

Family Laridae
Laughing Gull *(Larus atricilla)*
Herring Gull *(Larus argentatus)*
Arctic Tern *(Sterna paradisaea)*
Forster's Tern *(Sterna forsteri)*
Black Tern *(Chlidonias niger)*

Family Columbidae
Rock Dove *(Columba livia)*
Mourning Dove *(Zenaida macroura)*
Common Ground-Dove *(Columbina passerina)*

Family Cuculidae
Black-billed Cuckoo *(Coccyzus erythropthalmus)*
Yellow-billed Cuckoo *(Coccyzus americanus)*

Family Tytonidae
Barn Owl *(Tyto alba)*

Family Strigidae
Eastern Screech-Owl *(Otus asio)*
Great Horned Owl *(Bubo virginianus)*
Barred Owl *(Strix varia)*

Family Caprimulgidae
Common Nighthawk *(Chordeiles minor)*
Chuck-will's-widow *(Caprimulgus carolinensis)*
Whip-poor-will *(Caprimulgus vociferus)*

Family Apodidae
Chimney Swift *(Chaetura pelagica)*

Family Trochilidae
Ruby-throated Hummingbird *(Archilochus colubris)*

Family Alcedinidae
Belted Kingfisher *(Ceryle alcyon)*

Family Picidae
Red-headed Woodpecker *(Melanerpes erythrocephalus)*
Red-bellied Woodpecker *(Melanerpes carolinus)*
Yellow-bellied Sapsucker *(Sphyrapicus varius)*
Downy Woodpecker *(Picoides pubescens)*
Hairy Woodpecker *(Picoides villosus)*
Red-cockaded Woodpecker *(Picoides borealis)*

Northern Flicker *(Colaptes auratus)*
Pileated Woodpecker *(Dryocopus pileatus)*

Family Tyrannidae
Eastern Wood-Pewee *(Contopus virens)*
Acadian Flycatcher *(Empidonax virescens)*
Eastern Phoebe *(Sayornis phoebe)*
Vermilion Flycatcher *(Pyrocephalus rubinus)*
Great Crested Flycatcher *(Myiarchus crinitus)*
Western Kingbird *(Tyrannus verticalis)*
Eastern Kingbird *(Tyrannus tyrannus)*
Gray Kingbird *(Tyrannus dominicensis)*

Family Hirundinidae
Purple Martin *(Progne subis)*
Tree Swallow *(Tachycineta bicolor)*
Barn Swallow *(Hirundo rustica)*

Family Corvidae
Blue Jay *(Cyanocitta cristata)*
American Crow *(Corvus brachyrhynchos)*
Fish Crow *(Corvus ossifragus)*

Family Paridae
Carolina Chickadee *(Parus carolinensis)*
Tufted Titmouse *(Parus bicolor)*

Family Sittidae
Red-breasted Nuthatch *(Sitta canadensis)*
White-breasted Nuthatch *(Sitta carolinensis)*
Brown-headed Nuthatch *(Sitta pusilla)*

Family Certhiidae
Brown Creeper *(Certhia americana)*

Family Troglodytidae
Carolina Wren *(Thryothorus ludovicianus)*
Bewick's Wren *(Thryomanes bewickii)*
House Wren *(Troglodytes aedon)*
Winter Wren *(Troglodytes troglodytes)*
Sedge Wren *(Cistothorus platensis)*
Marsh Wren *(Cistothorus palustris)*

Family Muscicapidae
Golden-crowned Kinglet *(Regulus satrapa)*
Ruby-crowned Kinglet *(Regulus calendula)*
Blue-gray Gnatcatcher *(Polioptila caerulea)*
Eastern Bluebird *(Sialia sialis)*
Veery *(Catharus fuscescens)*
Gray-cheeked Thrush *(Catharus minimus)*
Swainson's Thrush *(Catharus ustulatus)*
Hermit Thrush *(Catharus guttatus)*
Wood Thrush *(Hylocichla mustelina)*
American Robin *(Turdus migratorius)*

Family Mimidae
Gray Catbird *(Dumetella carolinensis)*
Northern Mockingbird *(Mimus polyglottos)*
Brown Thrasher *(Toxostoma rufum)*

Family Motacillidae
American Pipit *(Anthus rebescens)*

Family Bombycillidae
Cedar Waxwing *(Bombycilla cedrorum)*

Family Laniidae
Loggerhead Shrike *(Lanius ludovicianus)*

Family Sturnidae
European Starling *(Sturnus vulgaris)*

Family Vireonidae
White-eyed Vireo *(Vireo griseus)*
Solitary Vireo *(Vireo solitarius)*
Yellow-throated Vireo *(Vireo flavifrons)*
Red-eyed Vireo *(Vireo olivaceus)*

Family Emberizidae

Subfamily Parulinae
Bachman's Warbler *(Vermivora bachmanii)*
Blue-winged Warbler *(Vermivora pinus)*
Golden-winged Warbler *(Vermivora chrysoptera)*
Orange-crowned Warbler *(Vermivora celata)*
Northern Parula *(Parula americana)*
Yellow Warbler *(Dendroica petechia)*
Chestnut-sided Warbler *(Dendroica pensylvanica)*
Magnolia Warbler *(Dendroica magnolia)*
Cape May Warbler *(Dendroica tigrina)*
Black-throated Blue Warbler *(Dendroica caerulescens)*
Yellow-rumped Warbler *(Dendroica coronata)*
Black-throated Green Warbler *(Dendroica virens)*
Blackburnian Warbler *(Dendroica fusca)*
Yellow-throated Warbler *(Dendroica dominica)*
Pine Warbler *(Dendroica pinus)*
Prairie Warbler *(Dendroica discolor)*
Palm Warbler *(Dendroica palmarum)*
Blackpoll Warbler *(Dendroica striata)*
Cerulean Warbler *(Dendroica cerulea)*
Black-and-white Warbler *(Mniotilta varia)*
American Redstart *(Setophaga ruticilla)*
Prothonotary Warbler *(Protonotaria citrea)*
Worm-eating Warbler *(Helmitheros vermivorus)*
Swainson's Warbler *(Limnothlypis swainsonii)*
Ovenbird *(Seiurus aurocapillus)*
Northern Waterthrush *(Seiurus noveboracensis)*
Louisiana Waterthrush *(Seiurus motacilla)*
Kentucky Warbler *(Oporornis formosus)*
Connecticut Warbler *(Oporornis agilis)*
Common Yellowthroat *(Geothlypis trichas)*
Hooded Warbler *(Wilsonia citrina)*
Canada Warbler (Wilsonia canadensis)
Yellow-breasted Chat *(Icteria virens)*

Subfamily Thraupinae
Summer Tanager *(Piranga rubra)*
Scarlet Tanager *(Piranga olivacea)*

Subfamily Cardinalinae
Northern Cardinal *(Cardinalis cardinalis)*
Rose-breasted Grosbeak *(Pheucticus ludovicianus)*
Blue Grosbeak *(Guiraca caerulea)*
Indigo Bunting *(Passerina cyanea)*
Painted Bunting *(Passerina ciris)*

Subfamily Emberizinae
Eastern Towhee *(Pipilo erythrophthalmus)*
Bachman's Sparrow *(Aimophila aestivalis)*
American Tree Sparrow *(Spizella arborea)*
Chipping Sparrow *(Spizella passerina)*
Field Sparrow *(Spizella pusilla)*
Vesper Sparrow *(Pooecetes gramineus)*
Lark Sparrow *(Chondestes grammacus)*
Savannah Sparrow *(Passerculus sandwichensis)*
Grasshopper Sparrow *(Ammodramus savannarum)*
Henslow's Sparrow *(Ammodramus henslowii)*
Le Conte's Sparrow *(Ammodramus leconteii)*
Fox Sparrow *(Passerella iliaca)*
Song Sparrow *(Melospiza melodia)*
Swamp Sparrow *(Melospiza georgiana)*
White-throated Sparrow *(Zonotrichia albicollis)*
Dark-eyed Junco *(Junco hyemalis)*

Subfamily Icterinae
Bobolink *(Dolichonyx oryzivorus)*
Red-winged Blackbird *(Agelaius phoeniceus)*
Eastern Meadowlark *(Sturnella magna)*
Rusty Blackbird *(Euphagus carolinus)*
Brewer's Blackbird *(Euphagus cyanocephalus)*
Boat-tailed Grackle *(Quiscalus major)*
Common Grackle (Quiscalus quiscula)
Brown-headed Cowbird *(Molothrus ater)*
Orchard Oriole *(Icterus spurius)*
Baltimore Oriole *(Icterus galbula)*

Family Fringillidae
Purple Finch *(Carpodacus purpureus)*
House Finch *(Carpodacus mexicanus)*
Pine Siskin *(Carduelis pinus)*
American Goldfinch *(Carduelis tristis)*

Family Passeridae
House Sparrow *(Passer domesticus)*

Appendix D

EMERGENCY ASSISTANCE

In most places, the nearest sheriff, ambulance, and fire department are just three keys away on the nearest telphone. Dial 911 and as calmly as possible describe the problem to the dispatcher. Clinch County (areas west of the refuge, including Fargo, Georgia) does not have 911 service. Emergency assistance can be obtained by calling the sheriff's department at 912-487-5315.

HOSPITALS

Camden Medical Center
2000 Dan Proctor Drive
St. Mary, GA 31558
(912) 576-4200

Clinch Memorial Hospital
524 Carswell Street
Homerville, GA 31634
(912) 487-5211

Charlton Memorial Hospital
1203 North Third Street
Folkston, GA 31537
(912) 496-2531

Satilla Regional Medical Center
410 Darling Avenue
Waycross, GA 31501
(912) 283-3030

Appendix E

NEARBY ACCOMMODATIONS AND SERVICES

The cities of Waycross and Folkston offer hotel and motel accommodations, grocery stores, gas stations, and restaurants. The city of Fargo offers restaurants, gas stations, and a grocery store. Five campgrounds operate in the vicinity of the refuge and are listed below.

Okefenokee Pastimes

R.R. 2 Box 3090
Folkston, GA 31537
(912) 496-4472 (voice/fax)

Okefenokee Pastimes is a privately operated campground located adjacent to the refuge's east entrance. The owners are skilled silversmiths and operate a studio on the premises. A small gallery offering work from southeastern artists is located in the main building.

Facilities: Cabins. Tent and RV campsites. Electric, water, and sewer hookups available. Restrooms. Showers. Fire rings. Reservations accepted.

Hours: Open year-round, but subject to seasonal closure. Call for confirmation. Office open until 9 P.M.

Location: Directly opposite the refuge's east entrance on Georgia 121/23.

Trader's Hill Recreation Area

(912) 496-3412

Trader's Hill Recreation Area is a no-frills publicly operated campground located on the banks of the St. Marys River 5 miles from the refuge's east entrance. This budget-priced campground has the added bonus of being just up the road from a free public boat ramp on the St. Marys. The only drawback to the boat ramp is that it is frequented by a variety of personal watercraft (jet ski) users and motorboat operators. The tent area does not have individually designated sites but rarely reaches full capacity.

Facilities: Tent and RV campsites. Electric and water hookups available. Dump station. Restrooms. Showers. Pay telephone.

Hours: Open year-round. Campground open from 7:30 A.M. until dark. Office generally open from 1 P.M. until dark.

Location: From the refuge's east entrance, follow Georgia 121/23 north for 3.5 miles to Tracy's Ferry Road. Turn right (east) onto Tracy's Ferry Road and proceed 1.5 miles to the campground.

Stephen C. Foster State Park

Route 1 Box 131
Fargo, GA 31631

(912) 637-5274

(800) 864-7275 (reservations only)

Stephen C. Foster State Park is a publicly operated state park located within the refuge at Billys Lake on the west side.

Facilities: Cottages. Tent and RV campsites. Electric and water hookups available. Restrooms. Showers. Washer and dryer. Pay telephone. Boat ramp. Canoe, motorboat, and bicycle rental. Museum. Interpretive Center. Guided tours. Small store.

Hours: Open year-round. Campground open 6:30 A.M.–8:30 P.M. from March 1 to September 14 and 7 A.M.–7 P.M. from mid-September to February 28. Office open 7 A.M.–6 P.M. from March 1 to mid-September and 8 A.M.–5 P.M. from mid-September to February 28.

Location: Within the refuge 17 miles northeast of Georgia 94/ U.S. Highway 441 on Georgia 177.

Griffis' Camp

R.R. 1 Box 139

Fargo, GA 31631

(912) 637-5395

Griffis' Camp is a "rustic," no-frills, privately operated campground on the Suwannee River located just outside the refuge's west entrance. Though there is a boat ramp, you can't access the refuge via the river without first obtaining a permit and carrying your boat across the Suwannee River Sill.

Facilities: Tent and RV campsites. Electric (limited) and water hookups available. Restroom. Showers. Boat ramp. Pay telephone.

Hours: Open year-round. Office open "most anytime."

Location: 10 miles northeast of Georgia 94/ U.S. Highway 441 on Georgia 177 (0.5 mile outside of the refuge's west entrance).

Laura S. Walker State Park

5653 Laura Walker Road

Waycross, GA 31503

(912) 287-4900

(800) 864-7275 (reservations only)

Laura S. Walker State Park is located north of the refuge and includes a publicly operated campground.

Facilities: Tent and RV campsites. Electric and water hookups available. Restrooms. Showers. Pay telephone. Boat ramp. Boat rental. Pool. Golf course.

Hours: Open year-round. Campground open 7 A.M.–10 P.M. Office open 7 A.M.–5 P.M.

Location: 9 miles southeast of Waycross on Georgia 177.

Index

Page numbers in *italics* refer to photo captions.

About the Authors

Elizabeth Anne Domingue is a wildlife biologist and an avid canoeist and wildlife photographer. She has studied amphibians in Great Smoky Mountains National Park; amphibians and reptiles in Florida; ground squirrels in Idaho; birds, amphibians, raccoons, and ticks in New York; and Eastern Phoebes in Indiana. She has studied, taught, and conducted research at Cornell University, Purdue University, and the University of Florida. She lives in Townsend, Tennessee.

David M. O'Neill is a self-described naturalist who has studied birds, butterflies, and mammals. He has also conducted environmental education programs and assisted with study of the hydrology and vegetation communities of the Okefenokee Wildlife Refuge.

FALCON GUIDES® are available for where-to-go hiking, mountain biking, rock climbing, walking, scenic driving, fishing, rockhounding, paddling, birding, wildlife viewing, and camping. We also have FalconGuides on essential outdoor skills and subjects and field identification. The following titles are currently available, but this list grows every year. For a free catalog with a complete list of titles, call FALCON toll-free at 1-800-582-2665.

Birding Guides
Birding Minnesota
Birding Montana
Birding Texas
Birding Utah

Field Guides
Bitterroot: Montana State Flower
Canyon Country Wildflowers
Great Lakes Berry Book
New England Berry Book
Pacific Northwest Berry Book
Plants of Arizona
Rare Plants of Colorado
Rocky Mountain Berry Book
Scats & Tracks of the Rocky Mtns.
Tallgrass Prairie Wildflowers
Western Trees
Wildflowers of Southwestern Utah
Willow Bark and Rosehips

Fishing Guides
Fishing Alaska
Fishing the Beartooths
Fishing Florida
Fishing Glacier National Park
Fishing Maine
Fishing Montana
Fishing Wyoming

Paddling Guides
Floater's Guide to Colorado
Paddling Montana
Paddling Okeefenokee
Paddling Oregon
Paddling Yellowstone & Grand
    Teton National Parks

Rockhounding Guides
Rockhounding Arizona
Rockhound's Guide to California
Rockhound's Guide to Colorado
Rockhounding Montana
Rockhounding Nevada
Rockhound's Guide to New Mexico
Rockhounding Texas
Rockhounding Utah
Rockhounding Wyoming

Walking
Walking Colorado Springs
Walking Denver
Walking Portland
Walking St. Louis

How-to Guides
Avalanche Aware
Backpacking Tips
Bear Aware
Leave No Trace
Mountain Lion Alert
Reading Weather
Wilderness First Aid
Wilderness Survival

More Guidebooks
Backcountry Horseman's
    Guide to Washington
Camping California's
    National Forests
Exploring Canyonlands &
    Arches National Parks
Exploring Hawaii's Parklands
Exploring Mount Helena
Recreation Guide to WA
    National Forests
Touring California & Nevada
    Hot Springs
Trail Riding Western
    Montana
Wild Country Companion
Wild Montana

■ *To order any of these books, check with your local bookseller*
*or call FALCON® at **1-800-582-2665**.*
Visit us on the world wide web at:
www.falconguide.com

FALCON®

HIKING GUIDES

Hiking Alaska
Hiking Alberta
Hiking Arizona
Hiking Arizona's Cactus Country
Hiking the Beartooths
Hiking Big Bend National Park
Hiking Bob Marshall Country
Hiking California
Hiking California's Desert Parks
Hiking Carlsbad Caverns
  and Guadalupe Mtns. National Parks
Hiking Colorado
Hiking the Columbia River Gorge
Hiking Florida
Hiking Georgia
Hiking Glacier & Waterton Lakes National Parks
Hiking Grand Canyon National Park
Hiking Grand Staircase-Escalante/Glen Canyon
Hiking Great Basin National Park
Hiking Hot Springs in the Pacific Northwest
Hiking Idaho
Hiking Maine
Hiking Michigan
Hiking Minnesota
Hiking Montana
Hiker's Guide to Nevada
Hiking New Hampshire

Hiking New Mexico
Hiking New York
Hiking North Cascades
Hiking Northern Arizona
Hiking Olympic National Park
Hiking Oregon
Hiking Oregon's Eagle Cap Wilderness
Hiking Oregon's Mount Hood/Badger Creek
Hiking Oregon's Three Sisters Country
Hiking Pennsylvania
Hiking Shenandoah
Hiking South Carolina
Hiking South Dakota's Black Hills Country
Hiking Southern New England
Hiking Tennessee
Hiking Texas
Hiking Utah
Hiking Utah's Summits
Hiking Vermont
Hiking Virginia
Hiking Washington
Hiking Wisconsin
Hiking Wyoming
Hiking Wyoming's Wind River Range
Hiking Yellowstone National Park
Hiking Zion & Bryce Canyon National Parks
The Trail Guide to Bob Marshall Country

■ *To order any of these books, check with your local bookseller
or call FALCON® at **1-800-582-2665**.*

Visit us on the world wide web at:
www.falconguide.com

FALCON™

WILDERNESS FIRST AID

By Dr. Gilbert Preston M.D.

Enjoy the outdoors and face the inherent risks with confidence. By reading this easy-to-follow first-aid text, all outdoor enthusiasts can pack a little extra peace of mind on their next adventure. *Wilderness First Aid* offers expert medical advice for dealing with outdoor emergencies beyond the reach of 911. It easily fits in most backcountry first-aid kits.

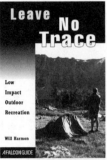

LEAVE NO TRACE

By Will Harmon

The concept of "leave no trace" seems simple, but it actually gets fairly complicated. This handy quick-reference guidebook includes all the newest information on this growing and all-important subject. This book is written to help the outdoor enthusiast make the hundreds of decisions necessary to protect the natural landscape and still have an enjoyable wilderness experience. Part of the proceeds from the sale of this book go to continue leave-no-trace education efforts. The Official Manual of American Hiking Society.

BEAR AWARE

By Bill Schneider

Hiking in bear country can be very safe if hikers follow the guidelines summarized in this small, "packable" book. Extensively reviewed by bear experts, the book contains the latest information on the intriguing science of bear-human interactions. *Bear Aware* can not only make your hike safer, but it can help you avoid the fear of bears that can take the edge off your trip.

MOUNTAIN LION ALERT

By Steve Torres

Recent mountain lion attacks have received national attention. Although infrequent, lion attacks raise concern for public safety. *Mountain Lion Alert* contains helpful advice for mountain bikers, trail runners, horse riders, pet owners, and suburban landowners on how to reduce the chances of mountain lion-human conflicts.

Also Available

• Wilderness Survival • Reading Weather • Backpacking Tips
• Climbing Safely • Avalanche Aware

To order check with your local bookseller or
call FALCON® at **1-800-582-2665.**

www.falconguide.com